D1583423

Alright Darlin

Cam x

Say What You Mean and Get What You Want

GEORGE R. WALTHER

Say What You Mean and Get What You Want

*How to speak the
language of success*

PIATKUS

This book is dedicated to my daughter, Kelcie Paige.

You will hear the sound of one man clapping.

Copyright © 1993 George R Walther

Reprinted 1997

First published in Great Britain by
Judy Piatkus (Publishers) Limited,
5 Windmill Street, London W1P 1HF

The moral right of the author has been asserted

*A catalogue record for this book is available from the
British Library*

ISBN 0 – 7499 – 1202 – 2
ISBN 0 – 7499 – 1203 – 0 (pbk)

Designed by Paul Sanders

Typeset in Compugraphic Sabon by
Action Typesetting Limited, Gloucester
Printed and bound in Great Britain by
Biddles Ltd, Guildford and King's Lynn

CONTENTS

ACKNOWLEDGEMENTS

This book is the direct result of enthusiastic feedback from clients, readers, users of my audio and video tapes, and audience members who asked for more of the concepts introduced in my book *Phone Power*. Thank you all for inspiring me to write *Say What You Mean and Get What You Want*.

It's a long way from concept to finished book. Adrienne Ingrum got me started by encouraging me to 'put it in writing'. My agents, Arthur and Richard Pine, handled the publishing negotiations and allowed me to concentrate on creating my best work. Laurie Larsen's nimble fingers and sharp eyes helped with much of the word processing. At Putnam, who originally published the book, my editorial team, Rena Wolner and Christine Pepe, provided superb support, expertly pared the manuscript, and helped me polish my writing.

Many colleagues in the National Speakers Association have provided priceless fellowship and professional support. I appreciate their abundant suggestions and assistance.

No author could ask for a better 'home team'. Thank you, Julie for your contributions of ideas and time. I respect and appreciate your rare and marvellous combination of raw brainpower and level-headedness. And most important of all, thank you for being such a wonderful mother to our daughter.

INTRODUCTION

Two employees, in adjacent offices, each tell their supervisors that they haven't completed their monthly reports on time:

Employee A says:

> 'Well, John, to tell you the truth, there were so many distractions this week that I just couldn't finish the report on time. It's not my fault. I couldn't help it. You know what I mean. I'm afraid I won't be able to get it done until the middle of next week.'

Employee B says:

> **'John, my monthly report isn't finished yet. We can review my summary of the main points together now, and I'll have the completed report for you before Thursday morning. I take responsibility for the delay. I decided that some of my other projects needed to be given higher priority.'**

Which employee has better career prospects?

You and a friend own identical cars, and they both start making peculiar squealing sounds somewhere in the engine. First thing on Monday morning, each of you takes your car to a different dealer.

Dealer A says:

> 'I'm afraid our service department won't be open until about 9 o'clock. It's Monday, you know. I can't help

you myself. I only work in the second-hand car sales department. You'll just have to call back a little later. Sorry.'

Dealer B says:

'I'll be glad to help you. The service department will be open by 9 o'clock. Meanwhile, I can take down all the details. That way you'll be all set when they open in a few minutes.'

Which garage is likely to end up with plenty of satisfied customers who recommend it to their friends?

You decide to computerise your home finances. You visit two computer suppliers to find out which personal accounting software will work best for you.

Salesperson A says:

'The problem is, there are so many different types of software, it's almost impossible to work out which one's right for you. I'd hate to see you get stuck with the wrong one. Let's see now, which might be the best software for me to sell you?'

Salesperson B says:

'The first step is to find out which type of software will best match your needs. I want to be sure that we select the software that you'll be happiest with. Let's talk about what you want the software to do, and then I'll recommend the best option.'

Which salesperson are you likely to buy your software from?

In each case, A conveyed the same basic information as B. Yet, you, as the supervisor, or car owner, or software shopper, reacted very differently to what they said.

The big distinctions lie in how A and B expressed themselves. They both used about the same number of words;

neither spoke more intelligently than the other. Yet, the impact of what they said differed dramatically.

All day, every day, people size **you** up, based on the way you talk. In these examples, B is clearly going to move ahead faster in his career, make customers happier, enjoy stronger friendships, and generate higher sales than A.

This book shows how to ensure that you're always in the 'B' position. The techniques you learn here will help you create consistently positive impressions on others. They can be applied equally well at home with family and friends, or at work with customers, supervisors and colleagues.

Use the words and phrases you read here and you will achieve greater professional success, more harmonious relationships with friends and colleagues, a happier family life, better emotional and physical health, and yes, you'll even make more money.

Learning to speak more positively isn't like studying Latin or German. There are no vocabulary tests. You already know all the words and phrases. You just need to learn how to put those everyday expressions together.

This book presents some simple ways to apply positive thinking theories to your life. In fact you can start reaping the benefits even before you finish reading this introduction.

I've gathered 50 specific expressions you can use to help make sure things go your way, and covered each one in its own chapter. You can begin with any of the 50, starting at the beginning or at the end. Or you can just keep flicking through the book, adopting phrase after phrase. When you spot a powerless expression that you recognise as part of your present daily speaking habits, read that chapter. If you notice a familiar phrase like 'I'll try', or 'That could be a problem', or 'To be honest', ask yourself, 'How is my use of that expression holding me back? What should I be saying instead?' Read that chapter immediately.

The 50 chapters are grouped into sections, each focusing on one of the traits shared by successful, happy people. Positive talkers, for instance, rebound resiliently from apparent setbacks. Section III, 'Rebound Resiliently', includes several examples of phrases you can use when things aren't quite going the way you'd like.

Every chapter deals with a specific, all-too-common phrase, and begins with personal anecdotes and stories about relevant encounters with clients, audience members, friends or family. Then there is an explanation of the rationale behind the positive alternative I've recommended.

Finally, each chapter concludes with a 'Quick Reference: What You Can Do Right Now' summary. Here you'll find common power*less* phrases that you may be using habitually and unwittingly, along with their recommended positive replacements.

So, let's start! Flick through the book right now. Find a powerless phrase that you know you sometimes use. Maybe it's 'I'll have to . . . .' Read Chapter 1 and decide to banish that phrase starting *now*. Purge it from your vocabulary. Today, begin substituting the phrase 'I'll be glad to . . .' and keep it up. Then, move on to another phrase that catches your interest. Don't worry about reading the chapters or sections in the correct order. Do read them all.

You're going to see immediate results. Creating long-term changes in your life by changing the way you speak isn't easy – and it's also not terribly difficult. Start with one phrase right now. Get those powerless phrases out of your vocabulary and start talking positively.

I. *PROJECT POSITIVE EXPECTATIONS*

THE most noticeable characteristic of positive talkers is that they project positive expectations, both for themselves and for others. You may be familiar with the concepts of positive thinking as described in Dr Norman Vincent Peale's classic book, *The Power of Positive Thinking*. As he put it, 'When you change your thoughts, you change your life.' But you can't just sit in a corner and think positively – that won't change your life. You need to interact positively with others. I agree with Dr Peale's advice about positive thinking, and recommend that you take one more step.

Positive talkers go beyond **thinking** positively – they **talk** postively, too. Notice the difference between a person who says, 'I can never remember anyone's name' and the person who says, 'I'm working on improving my memory.'

I recently had my house renovated, and I noticed that those contractors who said 'I'll try and get back to you by tomorrow' rarely did. Those who said 'I'll have an answer for you by 5 o'clock tomorrow' lived up to their promises. That's because the expectations they set didn't just influence me, the listener. They influenced themselves as well. When you set positive expectations for others, you're setting them for yourself, too. Making a commitment increases your reliability in the other person's eyes, and it also helps ensure that you follow through.

A manager of a public service company noticed that

her staff often revealed their low morale through their routine daily greetings. She'd overhear colleagues greeting each other with, 'Hello, how are you?' The most common responses were along the lines of, 'Oh, OK, I suppose' or 'Only four more days till the weekend.' She suspected that these comments made everyone feel depressed.

At the next staff meeting, she explained her theory and implemented a reward system to encourage positive responses. She designated certain people as 'mystery greeters', so that other employees wouldn't know when their responses were being assessed. The greeters asked colleagues how they were, and noted those who offered positive responses. Those who the 'mystery greeters' felt had contributed most to a positive atmosphere were recognised and rewarded with a small prize at the end of the day. The result?

'It made a huge difference almost overnight. Once people became aware of the effect their greetings and responses had on each other, I heard them saying things like: "Great!"' or "I'm fine. How are you?" and so on. They all started believing each other, and really did feel much better. You could easily gauge the difference in morale.'

In the following chapters you'll meet people who focus on affirmative language and action, who set optimistic expectations for themselves and others, and who think, speak and behave positively. They use language to help create success for themselves. You can too.

1. *I'll Be Glad To!*

The person you share an office with has gone to lunch without arranging for anyone to take her calls. You're working through lunch so you can go home a little early. Her phone, on the desk beside yours, rings and rings and rings. Annoyed, you finally decide to answer it.

Say out loud to yourself:

'I'll have to take a message and she won't get it for another hour or so.'

Now say:

'I'll be glad to take your message and I'll make sure she gets it before 1.30.'

Which will give the caller a more favourable impression? Which will make you feel better about taking the message?

'Good evening. Thank you for calling the GE Answer Centre. I'm Miss Cooley, how may I help you?'

The General Electric Answer Centre in the USA uses my positive talking techniques when training its employees. I like to call in anonymously from time to time and check to see how consistently the Centre's employees apply their training.

When my wife and I decided to buy a freezer, I called (anonymously, of course) the Answer Centre late one Sunday night for some information before visiting a supplier. I started by asking about energy consumption:

'Which type of freezer is more energy-efficient: upright or chest style?'

Miss Cooley didn't sound old enough to have bought many freezers herself, and I was a little sceptical about her firsthand knowledge.

'That's a good question. I'm being trained at present, and I'd like to compare the efficiency ratings of several models for you.'

7

She'd LIKE to? I'm used to people saying something more along the lines of,

'Well, I'm still only a trainee, so I can't tell you for sure. What I'll have to do is check the details of several models and see if I can work it out.'

Rather than making it sound like a burden, I got the feeling that Miss Cooley was actually looking forward to finding out the answer herself.

GE markets a line of Hotpoint freezers, so I asked for information about those models as well. 'I'll be glad to check on the Hotpoint models for you,' Miss Cooley said.

It was late on a Sunday night. How could she be so GLAD to help me?

She explained the various features, and then she gave me the address of a nearby supplier where I could compare several models.

I know GE makes good products, and I appreciate being able to get information whenever I want it, even if it's late at night. The icing on the cake is the extremely congenial way Miss Cooley and her colleagues respond to callers' questions.

The GE Answer Centre is one outstanding example of a company's commitment to providing customers with complete, accurate information and friendly human contact. One of General Electric's original reasons for establishing the Answer Centre was to 'put on a friendly face' for consumers who might perceive GE as a big, impersonal bureaucratic organisation.

What struck me most during my conversation with Miss Cooley was something very simple: her consistent use of phrases like 'I'll be glad to check that . . .' and 'I'll be happy to get that information.' In each case she communicated not just that she would get the information I needed, but that she'd do it with pleasure. Imagine working an eight-hour shift beside Miss Cooley. If you handle twelve calls an hour, and each one includes, on average, three requests for information, you have the opportunity to choose between saying, 'I'll **have to** look that up' and 'I'll be **glad to** look that up', 288 times each day. After hearing yourself say 'I'll have to' 288 times in a single shift, how are you likely to feel? Exhausted, irritable, put-upon? Would it make a difference if you kept hearing yourself say 'I'll be glad to' instead?

Indeed, it can make a big difference, as the training staff and management at GE can attest. Even after answering thousands of calls, GE staff are remarkably enthusiastic, cheerful and at the same time entirely professional. One reason for the excellent morale is the training department's emphasis on positive talking. From their first day, new employees are trained to deliver accurate information in an upbeat manner.

In the course of an average day, we all respond to many requests for information. Simply replacing one word changes the whole tone of the response. Saying 'I'll be **glad to** check those dates for you' not only projects a pleasant, cooperative attitude; it also makes you feel better.

Whether you're responsible for training employees in your own organisation or you are interested in making your dealings with friends, supervisors or customers more rewarding, take advantage of the benefits that result from substituting positive phrases like 'I'll be happy to' for burdensome ones like 'I'll have to'.

QUICK REFERENCE

What you can do right now:

Each time you begin to say 'I'll **have to**', substitute a phrase that shows you'll be **glad to**. Notice the difference it makes in your own mood and in others' attitudes towards you.

Instead of saying,

'I'm afraid I'll have to find out and call you back.'

Say,

'I'd like to find out and call you back.'

Instead of saying,

'I'll have to check your file.'

Say,

'I'll be glad to check your file.'

Instead of saying,

'I'll have to do it.'

Say,

'I'll be glad to do it.'

2. *Will You Try, or Will You DO it?*

Your garage has been a mess for months. Tools are jumbled on the workbench, boxes are overflowing with things that ought to be thrown out, and the floor is filthy. Your spouse asks you (again) to clear it up this weekend.

Say out loud to yourself:

'OK, OK, I'll try to do it before I go to the football match on Saturday.'

Now say:

'I will have cleaned it up by Saturday afternoon.'

Which promise will motivate you to get it done?

Jeff Salzman is the co-author of *Real World 101* and *CareerTracking*, both valuable guides for accelerating your success in business. He told me about an encounter with a lawyer that dramatised the difference between 'I'll try' and 'I will.'

Early in Jeff's advertising career, one of his clients was sued. The prosecuting lawyer wanted Jeff to give a statement. 'The game,' Jeff explained, 'is to make yourself as unavailable as possible so as to avoid helping the other side build its case.' The lawyer asked if Monday would be convenient for a meeting. Jeff was busy. How about Tuesday? Oh, gosh, meetings all day. The lawyer quickly realised that Jeff was being cagey, so he changed tactics and asked an open-ended question: 'So, Jeff, when will you give your statement?' Jeff couldn't maintain that he was 'too busy' forever, so he suggested, 'I'll try for the Friday after next.' The lawyer's response was to ask for a firm commitment: 'Do I have your word that you **will** make your statement the Friday after next?' Jeff thought to himself, 'He's got me! Once I've made a commitment and given my word, he's won the game.' Of course, Jeff honoured his commitment. And he also learned a lesson. Ever since that phone call, whenever he detects an indefinite 'I'll try . . .' in what somebody says he counters with, 'Do I have your word that you **will**?'

The person who benefits most when you say 'I will' is *you*. When you hear yourself making a firm commitment, you are more likely to follow through with action than if you say 'I'll try.' That's merely an abbreviated form of 'I'll give it a shot but I'm not making any promises – we'll just wait and see what happens.' Or, as Ken Blanchard and Norman Vincent Peale wrote in *The Power of Ethical Management*, 'Trying is just a noisy way of not doing something.'

QUICK REFERENCE

What you can do right now:

Tell yourself and everyone else what you **will** do, not what you'll **try** to do.

Instead of saying,

'I'll try to finish the market research analysis by the middle of the week.'

Say,

'I will complete the market research analysis no later than Wednesday afternoon.'

Instead of saying,

'I'll try to practise my putting three times a week to get ready for the golf tournament next month.'

Say,

'I will practise my putting three times a week and be ready for the golf tournament next month.'

Instead of saying,

'I'll try to do it.'

Say,

'I will do it.'

3. *Say What You Want to Do*

While handling your arrangements for a last-minute business trip, your travel agent suggests securing the hotel room with a credit card.

Say out loud to yourself:

'I'd hate to see you lose your room if the flight is delayed and the hotel assumes you're not coming.'

Now say:

'I want to make sure that your room will be held for you even if you arrive a little later than expected.'

Which version sounds more helpful? Which suggests a more optimistic outlook?

You hear some interesting excuses when you're a debt collector. I was coaching a seasoned collector named Sharon at one of Ford Motor Credit's branch offices when we encountered Leon D. This customer insisted that he was deceased, and had even signed a letter verifying his own demise!

Sharon showed me the extensive records of her previous conversations with Leon D., and his case was very sad indeed. He had purchased a new Ford pick-up truck and financed it through his dealer. Soon after his loan was approved, he developed a severe brain tumour that clouded his thinking. Sharon had confirmed his diagnosis with the Veterans Administration hospital and learned that his condition was life-threatening. Since it was impossible to reason was Leon, she phoned his wife and discovered that he was on strong medication, and was drinking heavily and behaving irrationally.

I listened while Sharon spoke to Leon's wife:

'Hello, Mrs D. This is Sharon at Ford Motor Credit. I'm calling because we still haven't received the overdue payments for your husband's truck, and now the computer shows that his insurance has been cancelled for non-payment. I'm afraid I can see no alternative but to have the vehicle repossessed unless you're willing to help.'

Sharon had already threatened Leon with repossession, and his response had been to hide the vehicle. Repossession agents had been to the house to look for the truck, but were unable to locate it. If Mrs D. wouldn't make the payments, Sharon hoped she would at least reveal where the truck was.

Unfortunately Mrs D. wasn't helpful:

'Go *ahead and do whatever you have to do. I can't talk to him. He's completely crazy. I have no influence over him. Take the truck if that's what you want to do.'*

Sharon pressed on and described the likely consequences:

'Mrs. D., a repossession is going to look very bad on your credit record and will remain on your file for years to come. You don't want that, do you?'

Mrs D. knew she wasn't legally responsible.

'Listen, *young lady, I didn't sign that contract and I'm not accountable for Leon's irresponsible behaviour. There's nothing I'm going to do to help you and I don't care*

13

what happens. Besides, the doctors say he's going to die any day. I have no money to pay you or anybody else. I'm barely able to pay the mortgage. But Leon does have an insurance policy. And when he dies, that's my only hope of keeping my home. I don't drive his truck, and I didn't sign for it, so why should I care what happens to it?'

Now, with all the cards on the table, Sharon didn't know what to say. She ended the conversation, having made no headway at all:

'Mrs D., it sounds as if you have enough problems to deal with. I'd hate to see them get worse because of a repossession and default on your husband's credit records, but if you won't help me, that's my only choice at this point.'

After the call, Sharon and I talked about the difference between an 'I'd hate to . . .' and an 'I want to . . .' approach. People don't want to hear bad news – in fact, they block it out. They reach a point where they think things simply cannot get any worse. Sharon's approach had this effect on Mrs D.

She had been unsuccessful using the negative strategy – 'If you don't act now, things will get even worse,' so I suggested that she use the positive 'I want to . . .' strategy.

The following week Sharon called Mrs D. again:

'Mrs D., I can understand the uncomfortable position you're in, considering your husband's poor health and difficult behaviour. My aim is to make things better for you, not worse. You're absolutely right, you have no legal responsibility to help me locate the truck for repossession. But I can help you avoid a potential problem. Because of your husband's cancelled car insurance, medical history and drinking behaviour, it's very likely that you would be sued if he injured or, heaven forbid, killed someone while driving the truck. I *want to* help you keep your home and make sure you receive the proceeds of your insurance. What I *can* do is ensure that Leon doesn't injure anyone. If you'll tell me where to find the truck,

I'll have it quietly removed and will tell nobody about our conversation. I'm sorry about the terrible situation you're in, and I *want to* help improve it.'

Mrs D. hadn't thought of it that way. She quickly told Sharon where Leon had hidden the truck and asked her to have it picked up as soon as possible.

As a precaution, Sharon phoned the local police and explained that Ford was about to repossess the vehicle. The police knew Leon well, and considered him to be extremely dangerous. The Chief of Police insisted on helping by sending three of his patrol cars to meet Sharon and the repossession agent. Ford avoided having to write off the vehicle, and they may well have saved Mrs D. a good deal of grief, as well as her husband's potential innocent victims. The 'I want to . . .' approach helped Sharon make the best of a bad situation.

Whenever you're motivating someone to do what you'd like them to do, focus on the desirable positive end result, not the negative alternative. Tell people what you **want to** do for them, not what you'd **hate to** do to them.

There are many opportunities to do this in your daily life. If you and your spouse are planning to attend your child's school play, and you're concerned about getting there in good time, you will generate more positive attention by saying:

'Let's both leave work a little early today. I *want to* be sure we're both there on time to *enjoy* Emily's performance in the school play.'

rather than,

'You'd better leave work a little early today. I'd *hate* you to get caught in traffic and *miss* Emily's performance in the school play.'

If you're talking to a customer about a special offer that expires at the end of the month, consider the more positive impact you will have by saying:

'I want to be sure we get your order processed before Friday so you can take advantage of the special offer we're running this month,'

instead of using the negative 'hate to' approach:

'I'd hate you to miss the special offer we're running this month, so you'd better make sure your order isn't late.'

Whenever you use a phrase like 'I'd hate to', you focus attention on the looming potential negative outcome you want to avoid. The image you project will be a positive one when you focus on the good results you are moving towards rather than the bad ones you are seeking to avoid.

QUICK REFERENCE

What you can do right now:

Use 'I want to' and describe the positive outcomes you have in mind, rather than saying what you'd 'hate to' have happen.

Instead of saying,

'We'd better leave for the airport a little early. I'd hate to miss the flight because we got caught in traffic.'

Say,

'Let's leave for the airport a little early. I want to be sure we get there in plenty of time for the flight.'

Instead of saying,

'I'd hate to see your credit record ruined by having you car repossessed and your account shown as a default.'

Say,

'I want to help you maintain a good credit record and ensure that your account shows a positive rating.'

Instead of saying,

'I'd hate to give you the wrong information.'

Say,

'I want to give you the right information.'

4. *I Haven't Yet and I CAN*

Your boss asks you to prepare a Lotus spreadsheet analysis and determine the company's present break-even point. You're not proficient with Lotus 1 – 2 – 3 or any similar spreadsheet software.

Say out loud to yourself:

'I can't do a spreadsheet analysis and I can't even work out Lotus 1 – 2 – 3.'

Now say:

'I haven't done a spreadsheet analysis before. I can start by learning to use Lotus 1 – 2 – 3.'

Which sounds like the employee who's going to make progress, learn new skills, and become an increasingly valuable asset to the company? Which lacks confidence, sounds stagnant and probably faces a rather limited future?

As Beth, my new hairdresser, began washing my hair, she started with the usual get-friendly-with-your-new-client opening question:

'So, George, what business are you in?'

Most people don't know any professional speakers, so I wasn't surprised at her reaction when I told her about my work:

'What? You mean you give speeches for a living? Oh, I would never do that. I'm OK in a one-to-one conversation, but it would be impossible for me to give a speech. In fact, one of my teachers used to get me to do all my oral presentations in writing because I just couldn't talk in front of the class. I even took a speech course once, but I got an F. I get all sweaty and my mind goes completely blank. No, I can't give speeches.'

Each time the subject of speaking has come up since her first oral presentation at school, Beth has repeated to herself and anyone listening: 'I can't give a speech.' Her mind has heard her own proclamation over and over again, and she's absolutely convinced it's true.

Beth talked (non-stop) through my shampoo, cut and blow-dry so I know she **can** speak. If there had been 50 other clients waiting for haircuts, all within earshot but out of sight, Beth would have been giving a speech without even knowing it.

To be accurate, she should have said,

'I haven't ever liked giving speeches.'

Or even,

'I don't like giving speeches, have always done badly in the past, and don't ever want to do it again. In fact, I feel scared stiff at the thought of facing a group of people and giving a speech.'

That might all be true, but for Beth to say she **can't** speak in front of a group is inaccurate and self-limiting.

There's very little that you or I absolutely can't do. I've never competed in Alaska's annual dog-sled race, don't like prolonged exposure to sub-zero temperatures, and do my best to avoid pain and suffering. I **can**, though, compete in a dog-sled race across Alaska. Of course I'd need years of training, substantial financial backing, and lots of other preparation; and I **can** compete in such a race. I don't want to and guarantee that I won't. But I **can**.

Whenever people tell you – or themselves – what they **can't** do, they're slamming shut the door that leads to their untapped potential. As I wrote this book, I often caught myself saying what it seemed like I **couldn't** do. On many mornings I thought to myself,

'I can't squeeze in more than two and a half or three hours of solid writing each day. At this rate I can't possibly finish the manuscript before my publisher's deadline.'

Well, you're reading the book and I did complete it on time. The correct statement would have been:

'I haven't yet exceeded three uninterrupted hours in my daily writing schedule. I am going to finish the manuscript on time, so that means I'll need to write for about six hours each day. Starting today, I can begin adjusting my schedule to leave more time for concentrated writing.'

When someone says 'I can't do that,' he is probably placing an inaccurate and counter-productive limitation on what he can accomplish. The word 'can't' acts as a self-fulfilling prophecy. If you say you can't accomplish something, that's like saying you never will. Since your mind likes you to be right, it works hard to ensure that you're correct when you say you 'can't'. It therefore undermines your effectiveness so you do not reach your goals, even if you attempt to do so.

QUICK REFERENCE

What you can do right now:

When describing your capabilities to yourself or to anyone else, eliminate 'I can't' from your vocabulary.
Instead of saying,

'I can't even break par on that golf course!'

Say,

'I haven't yet broken par, and I'm working on it.'

Instead of saying,

> 'There's no point looking at new houses. We can't even afford a maisonette. We'll be renting a lousy flat for the rest of our lives.'

Say,

> **'Considering our present financial situation, we can afford to buy a flat in two to three years. As the market adjusts, we'll be saving towards our deposit. Meanwhile, we can look at ways of trimming our expenditure.'**

Instead of saying,

> 'I can't do that.'

Say,

> **'I haven't yet done it and I can.'**

5. *Refuse to Be Helpless*

You've been feeling tired for months, and your doctor discovers that you have a rare bone marrow disease. Following an extensive course of treatment and hundreds of blood transfusions, the doctor tells you there is nothing further medical science can do to prolong your life.

Say out loud to yourself:

> 'I suppose that's it. If the doctors hold out no hope for me, I may as well give up. What's the point? I'm in pain and I'm going to die anyway.'

Now say:

> **'I don't accept that. My condition is not hopeless. I can and will improve the quality, if not the quantity, of my life.'**

Which sounds like the patient who will see little

improvement in his condition? Who has a fighting chance?

Michael Ballard's 'new life' began when his doctor, George P. Konok MD, said,

'I'm going to start your treatment from the neck down. You're going to finish it from the neck up.'

Michael was a successful account executive in the packaged goods retailing business. He became ill and was diagnosed as having inflammatory bowel disease, commonly known as colitis. Some of the unpleasant effects are emotional: worry, panic and embarrassment. It doesn't do much for your self-confidence to know that you could 'have an accident' at any time. The worst part was hearing a well-intentioned medical professional tell him, 'There is nothing that can be done for your condition.'

Colitis can have a particularly sinister consequence: it is often a precursor to cancer. Soon Michael was diagnosed as having cancer of the bowel near his liver. The doctors warned that his lymph glands could be next, and for cancer patients, that's usually the beginning of the end.

Along with this new diagnosis came a blessing in the form of his new physician, Dr Konok. He pulled a blackboard up to Michael's bedside and gave him a serious 'chalk talk', drawing diagrams of the various organs that were affected, showing Michael what the surgeons would do and explaining how the chemotherapy was supposed to work. After a careful, factual explanation of Michael's current condition, he gave him the prognosis. He tossed the chalk in the air and said,

'I can tell you the odds that are in the medical textbooks, but I want you to know that you make your own odds. I cannot guarantee that you can make yourself live any longer. I can absolutely guarantee that you can live a fuller life if you decide to. When you begin your chemotherapy, you will experience side effects. If you view this as a healing process, you will have a much

better experience than if you view it as a sickening one. I will treat you from the neck down. Your job is to treat yourself from the neck up.'

Michael's treatment proceeded, with three operations. After the third, supposedly final step in his course of treatment, he was informed that the operation had failed; the cancer was still spreading.

Michael had always used positive language in his professional life. Now, though, facing the biggest 'contest' of his life, he was using negative language, accepting the doctors' assessment that his situation was 'hopeless'. When they said, 'You can't change things', he believed them.

At this point, Michael Ballard decided that the same techniques which had brought him success in his sales career were his best hope for success in his life.

Home from the hospital between courses of treatments, he bought a new pair of running shoes to use as he became well again. He played positive music including 'The Rainbow Connection' and the theme from *Rocky*. He paced round the house in his new running shoes, reading favourite quotations from the *The Best of Success*. Michael's breakthrough came when he transferred the skills he had learned, mastered and benefited from in business to his personal health.

Today his doctor describes Michael Ballard as 'Dangerously fit. Able to leap tall buildings with a single bound, and very tall ones with a running start.'

He has had no sign of cancer for eight years, and has chosen not to have any for the rest of his life.

Michael Ballard now has a new profession. He runs seminars on using the power of language to help patients recover from their illnesses. He's determined to make doctors and nurses aware of how damaging their language can be for worried patients – and how powerfully helpful it can be when used positively.

He explains that the techniques and specific words he used won't work for everyone. In his volunteer work, patients often comment,

'*Michael, I can't say what you said. It doesn't feel right for me.*'

He answers,

'**Fine, put it in your own words, but keep the spirit. Repeat the positive affirmations that feel right for you. If you say nothing else, say "Oh, yes I can." Don't let anyone, medical professional or not, tell you that your situation is hopeless. You can always improve the quality of your life, even if you don't change the quantity of it.**'

If you are already threatened by a serious illness, please do not give up. You can fight. Your positive expectations will improve the quality of your life.

QUICK REFERENCE

What you can do right now:

If you feel sick, combine appropriate medical attention with personal action. Use your language to promote a positive attitude and strengthen your body's natural disease-fighting powers.

Instead of saying,

'I can't fight this. My condition is hopeless. The doctor said so.'

Say,

'**I can improve the quality of my life, and I will. The doctor doesn't realise how strong I am.**'

Instead of saying,

'My condition is hopeless; I can't change it.'

Say,

'**I can improve the quality of my life.**'

6. *Better When Than If*

Your child is unenthusiastic about his French classes and finds it difficult to complete his homework each night. Tonight you use a reward to encourage him to finish.

Say out loud to yourself:

'If you finish your French homework, you can have a big helping of that new French vanilla ice cream I bought today.'

Now say:

'When you finish your French homework tonight, we'll all have a big helping of that new French vanilla ice cream I bought today.'

Which sounds as if you really expect him to finish his homework? Which shows that you aren't at all sure he's going to?

You've probably noticed shopkeepers becoming more environmentally conscious lately. Some supermarkets put on special labels indicating products that use recycled packaging, those that are biodegradable, and so on. Some of the shops offer a few pence off your bill when you bring in your own shopping bag. Some have a small bin for depositing plastic bags to be recycled. All those plastic bags are a threat to our environment because they can last for centuries. Recycling also saves trees and oil.

When I began writing this book, our local Safeway had no provision for recycling plastic bags. My wife decided to change that. She said to the person at the checkout, 'I really appreciate the efforts you've made to be environmentally conscious. When will you start recycling plastic bags?'

Not 'Do you think you could', not 'Would you consider', not 'It might be nice if you . . .', but 'WHEN WILL YOU?'

The staff member responded:

'Good question. I'll talk to the manager myself before the end of my shift. We should be recycling plastic bags. It won't take long to organise it.'

Our local Safeway now has a plastic bag recycling bin. If your supermarket doesn't yet, ask a 'When Question', not an 'If Question', next time you're shoppping.

When some of the major American banks want to improve their debt collectors' effectiveness, they call in Bill Arnold, Principal of the International Collection Training Institute. His job is to show people how they can project positive expectations onto others. Consider the difference between saying,

> 'I'll tell you what: if you can pay this overdraft off by the end of the week, I'll waive the charges.'

and

> **'Bring in a cheque for £67.50 before the end of the week, and I will waive the charges. When can you come in before Friday so I can credit your account?'**

Bill goes beyond the typical question, 'Do you think you could possibly pay this off by the end of the week?' He projects the positive expectation that the debtor will pay. His goal is to finalise the schedule for doing so, not to find out if it's going to happen.

If the debtor says, 'Wait a minute. I didn't say I was going to pay by the end of the week,' Bill backtracks to establish the basis for his positive expectation:

> 'Richard, I'm sure you are an honest and responsible person, aren't you?'
> 'Of course I am.'
> 'And you do want to honour your obligations, don't you?'
> 'Well, yes.'
> 'So you'd like to settle this by the end of the week, wouldn't you?'
> 'Yes, but I don't have enough money at the moment.'

Once again Bill steps past the 'iffy' questions and projects a positive expectation. Rather than saying,

'Well, when do you think you might have enough to pay it off?'

he presumes that the debtor wants to make headway as quickly as possible. He asks,

'How much are you going to be short of the £67.50 that's due this week?'

In other words, Bill doesn't ask **if** the debtor will pay; he moves on to the next question, **when** will he pay? And if the debtor says he doesn't have enough to pay it all now, Bill doesn't ask when he will, he asks **how much** he **will** pay right now.

When you want someone to take action, ask a logistical question. Not 'If' but 'When and how much?'

QUICK REFERENCE

What can you do right now:

When you hear yourself starting to ask a conditional 'If . . .' question, rephrase it to incorporate your positive expectation.

Instead of saying,

'We like the new park area you've provided for residents on the estate, but it's awfully rocky. We're wondering if it would be possible to have the rocks removed and the surface smoothed?'

Say,

'We like the new park area you've provided for residents on the estate. When will you have the rocks removed and the surface smoothed?'

Instead of saying,

'I know your engineers are probably very busy, but we need our phones fixed quickly. Do you think you could send someone over sometime today?'

Say,

> 'I know your engineers are very busy and I appreciate your help. Since these phones are a crucial link with our customers, we need them repaired fast. What time this afternoon can you have someone here?'

Instead of saying,

> 'I was wondering if you could . . . ?'

Say,

> 'When will you . . . ?'

7. It's No Problem!

Your local youth club organiser has fallen ill and you've just been asked to stand in for him at very short notice.
Say out loud to yourself:

> 'Sixty teenagers in one room, and I'm going to be responsible for maintaining order? It's going to be a terrible problem!'

Now say:

> 'Sixty teenagers in one room, and I'm going to be responsible for maintaining order? It's going to be an interesting challenge!'

Which version presupposes that things will go badly? Which suggests that you'll work out a creative way to handle the situation?

The Master of Ceremonies introduced Sonny Hendrix as he wheeled himself to the centre of the stage to deliver his speech. Everyone in the audience could see that Sonny's body was somewhat asymmetric, his arms and legs positioned oddly as he sat in his wheelchair. He didn't hold his head up quite straight, and there was something unusual

27

about the way he spoke. Many in the audience must have been thinking, 'And I thought I had problems. Sonny's entire existence in that wheelchair must be one big problem.'

Sonny doesn't see it that way.

I met him at the most inspiring graduation ceremony I've ever attended. It took place at the Resource Centre for the Handicapped, or RCH, near my home in Seattle. A former primary school, deemed unnecessary several years ago, has been converted into a learning centre dedicated solely to people with special physical needs.

RCH students are not content to just sit back and receive public assistance. They want to be active, contributing members of the workforce and they enrol in rigorous business and vocational courses with the aim of securing employment and becoming self-sufficient. The project is entirely supported by volunteers and commercial sponsors.

The evening began with guest speakers representing a few of the corporations that support the Centre: The Boeing Company, John Fluke Manufacturing, GTE, Digital Equipment Corporation, and so on. Not one speaker during the entire evening used the word 'problem'. It would have been so easy to describe these students as people beset with problems: limited mobility, public ignorance and many forms of prejudice.

Nobody mentioned 'problems'. They all talked about 'challenges'. Frank Shrontz, Chairman and CEO of Boeing, noted that his company employs 10,000 people with 'medical challenges' rather than 'disabilities'. Instead of referring to the graduates as people whose 'problems' entitle them to pity or special consideration, he pointed out that Boeing's employment policies have been formulated in the company's own best interests. 'When we find individuals like these, who have overcome significant challenges, we see people who have courage and perseverance. They make great employees.'

Sonny Hendrix was one of the student speakers. He had completed the Centre's 'TeleProfessionals' course, emphasising telemarketing and customer-service telephone skills. Addressing his fellow graduates, speaking into the microphone that was held for him beside his wheelchair, he said:

'Our disabilities are only equal to the barriers or doors we allow to be placed in front of us. We are responsible for our challenges.'

Sonny wasn't willing to accept the idea that a handicapped person faces problems and that most doors are closed to him. After the ceremony I talked to him about 'problems' and 'challenges'. He made a very definite distinction:

'A problem is something you hate. A challenge is something you want to overcome.'

One of my clients is a manager at a large telephone company. She noticed that the supervisors who worked for her often ask her for solutions to their problems, This practice wasn't helping to prepare them for career advancement, and left her with little time to handle her other responsibilities. She wanted to maintain her 'open door' policy, but she noticed that she'd often reach the end of the day feeling that she had accomplished little, except for extinguishing many small fires.

Her solution to this 'problem' was to talk to all the supervisors who reported to her and institute a new 'solution policy'. She reaffirmed her willingness to advise the supervisors individually whenever they felt the need. However, she asked them to change their approach. Supervisors were forbidden to use the word 'problem', and were also prohibited from starting the discussion until they had at least one solution in mind.

The old way:

'Excuse me, Katherine, I need to talk to you. I have a problem with Dennis Swall. He's been late for three days in a row now, and he's setting a very bad example for others. What should I do about it?'

The new way:

'Excuse me, Katherine, I'd like to tell you about an idea I've had for improving Dennis Swall's punctuality. Please tell me if you can suggest an even more effective approach.'

The result? Katherine did her supervisors a great service by encouraging them to be self-reliant. She was still able to ensure that the solutions they wanted to implement were appropriate, and everyone felt less depressed. Rather than being inundated with burdensome 'problems', Katherine and her supervisors used their meetings to discuss the relative merits of various positive solutions.

The same problem/solution substitution will work in your personal life too. When friends or family members start talking about 'problems', help them by shifting the discussion towards solutions. This will keep you focused on challenging opportunities rather than depressing problems.

QUICK REFERENCE

What you can do right now:

Substitute 'challenge' or 'opportunity' for 'problem' and concentrate on exploring solutions.

Instead of saying,

'Now that Jason is a teenager, we're having all kinds of problems with him.'

Say,

'We face some new challenges, now that Jason is a teenager.'

Instead of saying,

'The recent international crises have disrupted the currency exchange markets and caused all kinds of problems.'

Say,

'The recent currency fluctuations have opened up lots of new opportunities.'

Instead of saying,

'I'm afraid that's going to be a problem.'

Say,

'That sounds like a challenging opportunity.'

8. *Self-Fulfilling Prophecies Come True*

After finally becoming adept with the telephone system used in your department, you're transferred to another building, where a totally different system is used.

Say out loud to yourself:

'Oh no! I'm terrible with anything technical. It was bad enough finding out out how to transfer calls from my old phone. I'll never learn a whole new system.'

Now say,

'I became proficient with the phones we used before, and I know I can do just as well with the new system. I'll get some coaching from my colleagues and pick up one of those quick-reference cards to keep handy.'

Which sounds like someone who is doomed to cutting off callers with his new phone? Who's going to apply himself and learn the new system quickly?

Somehow, over the last few years, I have convinced myself that I'm terrible at following directions. The curious thing is that I've travelled extensively without ever getting lost. I've hitch-hiked from Nairobi to Cape Town, trekked into the Highlands of New Guinea, and followed ancient unmarked Inca trails in the Andes. I always reached my intended destination without any problems.

Yet I've recently become notorious for getting lost in my very own town. Our friends Lou and Vanna Novak recently invited us to dinner at their home, just 25 minutes away from ours. Before leaving the house, I phoned Vanna and said,

'I realise we've been to your place twice before, but I think you'd better give me the directions again. You know how I'm always getting lost.'

I went through the motions of writing down her instructions, but I didn't take the trouble to make sure of the details, expecting that I'd get lost anyway. Sure enough, half an hour after we were supposed to have arrived for dinner, I called on the car phone.

'Lou, we're lost. I have no idea what happened. I watched for the Magnolia Street Bridge, just as Vanna said, but somehow we ended up on the Ballard Bridge, and now I'm not even sure which side of the canal we're supposed to be on. I always get lost coming to your house.'

I felt so foolish. Our infant daughter was screaming in her car seat, and my wife Julie was in the back seat, looking after the baby and telling me off for confusing Vanna's instructions. We finally arrived (45 minutes late) only after Lou 'talked me in' on the car phone as I drove. It was like one of those old-fashioned movie scenes where the pilot of a small plane has a heart attack and his passenger guides the plane in to land by listening to radioed instructions from the tower.

On the way home Julie pointed out that, right from the start, I had set myself up to get lost. There was no way I **wouldn't** get lost. I'd programmed Lou and Vanna **and myself** for the eventual outcome by saying, 'I'm always getting lost.'

I have a compass. I'm reasonably intelligent, carry a detailed map, and I'm a skilled communicator. There's no logical reason for me ever to get lost. Why create artificial limitations on my own abilities? As of now, I've decided to stop saying, 'I always get lost.' Instead, I'll listen carefully to instructions, make careful notes, and say, 'I'll find it easily.'

What are your self-imposed limitations? What have you convinced yourself you're not good at? What myths do you perpetuate by telling others you lack certain talents?

'I'm all thumbs when it comes to fixing things.'
'I've never been able to cook.'
'Study French? What's the point? I'm terrible with languages.'

I have decided today, as I write, to unlock my talent for finding my way anywhere. I invite you to decide, today, as you read this page, to unlock more of your talents. Stop telling yourself and others that you're 'not good at' something, and find out how good you truly are.

QUICK REFERENCE

What you can do right now:

Replace habitual self-limiting phrases with empowering assertions.

Instead of saying,

'I've always had trouble with maths. I'm just no good with numbers. I can never work out percentages, even with a calculator.'

Say,

'I do lots of mathematical things well. I'm going to visit the library and refresh my memory of basic calculations, like working out percentages.'

Instead of saying,

'I'm no good at that.'

Say,

'I'm getting better at that.'

9. *Get a Return on Your Investments*

You sell advertising space for a leading nature magazine, and you are meeting a businesswoman who wants to market a special high-tech bird-feeder. The potential advertiser has only just started her business, working from her kitchen table.

Say out loud to yourself:

'I realise that spending £300 on a magazine ad is a big commitment. It's hard to tell, of course, but you could get hundreds of orders.'

Now say:

'This ad represents a £300 investment. Let's look at the return that will generate, even if the response is only half of one per cent of our readers.'

Which approach is most likely to catch the entrepreneur's interest? Which sounds like the wiser allocation of funds?

I recently became a father, and I've since been advised by many other parents to 'spend as much time as possible' with my child while she's still very young. Sometimes, large parts of my day pass when I've done nothing except play with, talk to, adore and love our little baby. My wife does the same. I don't think of it as 'spending' time with her. We're 'investing' our time. I enjoy a big return: I know I'm a happier, more productive person when I take time off to enjoy Kelcie, and I also believe that for her whole lifetime, she'll benefit from getting a lot of high-quality attention from her parents.

There may be times as you read this book when you think I'm making too much of semantics. This could be one of those times. Consider the important influence your words have on your thinking.

Let's start with a dictionary definition:

spend: 1: TO PAY OUT (money, wealth, etc.) 2: TO CONCENTRATE (time, effort, thought, etc.) upon an object, activity, etc. 3: TO PASS (time) in a specific way, activity, place, etc. 4: TO USE UP COMPLETELY 5: TO GIVE UP (one's blood, life, etc.) in a cause.

Now, let's go back to the 'I's.

invest: 1: to commit (money) in order to earn a financial return 2: to make use of for future benefits or advantages

That's more like it. When I use my time to be with my daughter, I'm doing it because I expect benefits and advantages. I feel good and so does she.

Are you investing enough time with your family? Would the 'pay-off' make it worth increasing your stake?

In business, when you decide to commit limited funds to buy computers, employ people, or pay the rent, you do it because you expect the company to get a return on its investment. You don't spend on advertising, promotion and company vehicles – you invest.

Consider substituting 'invest' for 'spend' in your personal life. I've found there are quite a few times when 'spending' is appropriate. If I go to a fair and buy some candyfloss, I'm not making an investment. I buy some things just because I want them at the time. However, when it comes to buying a car, or choosing which washing machine to buy, or adding to my wardrobe, I like to think of my purchases as 'investments'.

Thinking – and talking – about 'investing' creates a consciousness of plenty rather than scarcity. If you're always spending, you're continually depleting limited resources. When you invest, you apply some of your resources with the expectation that you'll create more of them.

When you describe how you'll use your time, money and energy, talk in terms of investing. Use your resources wisely to generate a return, whether that means short-term satisfaction, long-term financial rewards or just a sense of having done the right thing.

QUICK REFERENCE

What you can do right now:

Substitute 'invest' for 'spend' when you talk about how you'll use your time, money and other resources.

Instead of saying,

'We're going to spend more money on our house and add a conservatory outside the kitchen.'

Say,

'We're going to invest in a conservatory to make our home more pleasant. When we move, it'll be a good selling feature too.'

Instead of saying,

'We can't afford to spend any more money on office furniture at the moment. Your department is going to have to make do with the desks and chairs we already have.'

Say,

'We're not going to buy any new furniture at the moment. While investing in more ergonomic chairs and tables could result in higher productivity, we believe other investments will provide a better return at present.'

Instead of saying,

'With autumn approaching, it's time to spend yet more money on clothes. I need a new coat, new shoes and, while I'm at it, I'll have to buy some new trousers too.'

Say,

'I'm going to invest in a new wardrobe for autumn and winter. I'll choose a good coat to keep me warm and comfortable, and some smart shoes and trousers to help me look my best at work.'

Instead of saying,

'I'm going to spend some time and money taking evening classes.'

Say,

'I'm going to invest some time and money in taking evening classes so I'm ready to progress in my career.'

10. *Nothing's Impossible*

You've already achieved terrific sales and your performance is nearly 20 per cent ahead of the same period last year. The regional manager compliments you on your performance and informs you that your target for the next quarter has just been increased by 25 per cent.

Say out loud to yourself:

'That's impossible! I'm working at top speed already, and I was lucky to get a few big orders in the first quarter. That's why I'm 20 per cent ahead of target now. There's no way I can close the year with a 25 per cent increase.'

Now say:

'That's going to be a challenge. A combination of circumstances has helped me make my current 20 per cent gain. You can continue relying on my total commitment for the rest of the year. I'll do my best to meet the new target, but I don't think the 25 per cent increase is realistic.'

Which sounds like the person who's going to have a shot at hitting 25 per cent?

Reverend Robert Schuller's Crystal Cathedral in Southern California is famous in America. I was lucky enough to be among the architecture buffs who toured the cathedral when its designer, Philip Johnson, officially unveiled his gem to the architectural community. I later learned the 'inside story' behind the construction of this impressive edifice.

When he first contacted Philip Johnson, Dr Schuller explained that he wanted to build a dramatic cathedral constructed entirely of glass, with outstanding acoustics and an unobstructed view of the pulpit from every single seat. This kind of building had never been constructed before, and required vast amounts of special glass and innovative construction techniques. On top of that, Southern California is one of the world's most active earthquake zones. As he explained his vision of the Crystal Cathedral to Mr Johnson, Dr Schuller added a special challenge: he had no money.

Mr Johnson looked at him and said,

'Wait a minute, let me get this straight. You want to erect a huge building the likes of which the world has never seen. You want it to be constructed using materials and techniques never before employed, and you have absolutely no money? That's impossible!'

Smiling, Reverend Schuller asked Philip Johnson to open the large dictionary kept on a pedestal in his office and look up the word 'impossible'. Mr Johnson walked across the room and began flicking through the pages. After a moment of confusion, the famous architect looked up and said, 'There's no "impossible" in this dictionary.'

There was Dr Schuller standing beside his desk, wearing an impish grin and holding a scalpel. He explained to the puzzled architect that he uses his blade to remove that negative word from any dictionary that crosses his path.

'Anything is possible,' says Dr Schuller.

There are very few things that are truly 'impossible'. Difficult, demanding, challenging, never-before-achieved — but not impossible. Why prejudice your own expectations by labelling a lofty aspiration 'impossible'?

Most of the great figures in history have had little use for the word 'impossible'. Did Columbus say it was impossible to sail to another continent? Did Kennedy say it was impossible to put an American astronaut on the moon? They faced daunting initial challenges and many setbacks along the way, but they did not label their goals 'impossible'.

The single worst effect of deciding that something is 'impossible' is that you don't give your efforts a fair chance. As we've seen before, your mind likes to make sure you're right. When you've convinced yourself that a thing is so, you set about proving it.

If you tell yourself it's impossible to wake up an hour early to work out a realistic family budget, it is. You sleep a little too long, you feel groggy rather than alert, and you decide to put off working on the budget until some other time. If you had woken up bright and early, and got straight to work producing a realistic budget, you would have proved your earlier self-assessment wrong. Your mind doesn't like you to be wrong, so it goes to work proving you were right all along.

When you tell yourself,

'I will wake up refreshed, an hour earlier than usual, and use that time to start working out a realistic family budget,' your mind, again, sets out to prove you right.

When you eliminate 'impossibility thinking', you open doors to achieve goals you never thought possible. Let your mind get busy proving you're right about what you decide is possible, instead of confirming your assessment of what you've deemed impossible.

QUICK REFERENCE

What you can do right now:

Banish the word 'impossible' from your vocabulary. Substitute a more accurate and positive phrase to describe what does not appear feasible.

Instead of saying,

'I realise that you want to earn enough money to buy yourself a car this summer, but it's impossible. And the cost of the insurance would be outrageous.'

Say,

'I know you'd like to have your own car, and it will take a lot of money to buy one and then make sure you have adequate insurance cover. Let's work out a realistic plan and discuss it with your father tonight. If this summer doesn't seem realistic, let's see about aiming for Christmas.'

Instead of saying,

'Get promoted to account executive before the end of the year? That's impossible! I'd need at least a year's

experience and there are already two other sales assistants
in line for the next promotion.'

Say,

'**As far as I know, nobody has yet been promoted to
account executive in under a year. I want to be the first.
I'm going to work as hard as I can to build up a really
outstanding performance record.**'

Instead of saying,

'This is impossible.'

Say,

'**This is going to require some special effort, and it can
be done.**'

11. *Kids Are All Ears*

It's a hot summer's day and your hefty teenager joins in with
some younger children down the street as they slide on
some wet plastic sheeting stretched across their front lawn.
When your son runs and slides, his mass and momentum
combine and he shoots off the plastic sheeting, levelling your
neighbour's gladioli and snapping off one of their automatic
sprinkler system's plastic attachments.

Say out loud to yourself:

'John! What's the matter with you? Now look what you've
done! You've wrecked the Smiths' front garden. You never
act your age. You're going to get in trouble all your life,
aren't you?'

Now say:

'**John! It looks as if you're going to be doing some
gardening. I know you mean well. The fact is you're
getting too big to play with young children's toys.**'

Which sounds like a parent who'll encourage his child
to use good judgement and grow gracefully into young

adulthood? Whose child is likely to end up lacking in self-confidence?

When little Julie was only six years old, she had a very short attention span. She had little interest in school and failed her third year exams. By the fourth year, her performance had improved very little, so her teacher conferred with her understandably concerned parents. 'You might as well face it', he informed them, 'Julie will never be any more than an average student.'

It's amazing how perceptive young children are. Although Julie doesn't remember her teacher ever directly giving her this discouraging assessment, she somehow got the message.

Julie performed very averagely all through primary and junior school. Always insecure about her mediocre academic performance, she formed most of her friendships with people who didn't excel in anything. They expected little of her, and that's what she delivered.

In her ninth year, Julie contracted mononucleosis and stayed home in bed for nine weeks. With few distractions, she threw herself into catching up on the schoolwork that she was missing by being out of class. For the first time she discovered that with some hard work she could be an A student and not an average one.

Twenty years later, a veterinarian noticed how Julie, at age 33, loved caring for horses. He told her she had a gift for diagnosing diseases and encouraged her to go to college, saying she was too clever not to. For some reason she believed him. Enrolled in some of the nearby college classes (and no longer burdened by the belief that she is destined to be 'nothing more than average'), she's doing much better.

Julie's father is Zig Ziglar, one of the best-known professional sales trainers and speakers in the world. I first heard Julie Ziglar Norman's story over lunch with Zig and his wife, Jean. My wife and I had our then three-month-old baby, Kelcie, with us and I asked Zig for some advice about what messages we should be giving our little girl during the most formative stage of her life. Zig is the author of *Raising Positive Kids in a Negative World*, an outstanding book that every parent should read. In it, Zig cites an anonymous quotation:

> ### Your Home Is Bugged!
> *In every home there are two microphones per child – one in each ear. These highly sensitive instruments pick up the table prayers, the songs sung, ordinary conversation, and all types of language. These all-hearing microphones transmit all they hear to highly impressionable minds. These sounds then become the vocabulary of the child and the basis for action.*

I know from personal experience that children are highly susceptible to negative messages. I was told I had Dumbo ears as a kid, and even though the rest of my body eventually caught up, I saw myself as an ugly person right up until my late 20s. Whenever I looked in a mirror, it was as if the image was peculiarly distorted – like one of those weird fairground mirrors with two convex bulges – all I could see were those two huge, unbecoming ears.

What you say, and what others say, has a very powerful influence on your child's self-image. A bruised self-image will take years to heal, if it ever does.

Dr Wayne Dyer, in his wonderful book *What Do You Really Want for Your Children?*, reminds all parents that they may be inadvertently lowering their children's sense of self-confidence and self-worth. One common mistake is to tell kids that they are bad children, when the truth is that they are good children behaving badly. It may sound like there's not much difference between:

> 'You bad girl! You've ruined the wallpaper by drawing on it with those crayons. Why are you so destructive?'

and,

> 'Drawing on the walls is bad. Now you've ruined our wallpaper. That was very destructive.'

While there is a huge difference in the psychological effects those two admonitions create, children are not yet able to grasp such subtle distinctions. We adults must take responsibility for making our approval of the child, and disapproval of the action, ultra-clear.

Kids also shape their futures with their own language. When you hear your child say,

'I always muck up my arithmetic. I'm stupid with numbers. I don't want to take the test. I have a tummyache,'

nip that powerless language in the bud:

'Jenny, you're very good with numbers. You're quite clever at working out how much change you should get when I give you a pound to buy some fruit. You can do really well in this arithmetic test. Let's practice together right now.'

I take Zig Ziglar's and Wayne Dyer's advice seriously. Though my little Kelcie doesn't talk yet, I'm sure she understands my feelings, if not my words. I will never let half a day pass without reminding her that she is a good, clever, beautiful person with a wonderful and rewarding life ahead of her.

Teaching your children to be positive talkers is one of the most wonderful gifts you can give. Show them by your own example that you project positive expectations, for them and for yourself. And keep in mind that any children you interact with, whether they're relatives, neighbours or kids you talk to for a few minutes while waiting in line at the supermarket or sitting on an aeroplane, are taking in every word you say. We reap what we sow.

QUICK REFERENCE

What you can do right now:

Be especially conscious of positive talking whenever you are with youngsters. Set an example and help shape kids' futures by speaking positively to and about them.

Instead of saying,

'You bad boy! You knocked over Mummy's vase and broke it.'

Say,

'When you run in the house, it's easy to break things accidentally. Please don't. Keep on being such a good runner, and always run outside from now on.'

Instead of saying,

'Oh, kids, I'm sorry we can't go to EuroDisney, but we can't afford it. Daddy's not very good at keeping jobs, and he got fired again.'

Say,

'Kids, we're going to change our plans to go to EuroDisney next year, when you're a little bigger and you can go on more of the rides. Daddy's going to make an exciting change and get a new job he'll like better than his old one. We're going to save up the money and really look forward to an even better holiday.'

Instead of saying,

'You're a bad child and you're always getting into trouble.'

Say,

'You're a good child, and that behaviour is not acceptable.'

II. *GIVE CREDIT WHERE IT'S DUE*

POSITIVE talkers give credit wherever credit is due. They don't hesitate to applaud others when they succeed, and they also give themselves credit whenever they create positive events in their own lives.

The effect your way of speaking can have on your life has been carefully researched, and the results are dramatic. Dr Martin Seligman, a psychologist at the University of Pennsylvania, has done outstanding work on the subject. The results of his research are summarised in his book, *Learned Optimism*.

Dr Seligman has identified three main indicators of optimism and pessimism in a person's common daily language or 'explanatory style'. When faced with positive events, optimists describe them using 'universal', 'internal' and 'permanent' terms. Powerless pessimists tend to attribute positive events to 'specific', 'external' and 'temporary' factors.

'Universal' means that you notice your success not just in one particular instance, but in all aspects of your life. 'Specific' explanations mean that you see positive situations as isolated events.

'Internal' terms indicate that you take personal responsibility, that you recognise your own role in bringing about positive outcomes, and give yourself credit for it. An 'external' explanatory style means that you attribute the success to something beyond your control — to 'a lucky break'.

'Permanent' descriptions identify positive events as continuing evidence of your regular pattern of success. A 'temporary' description says it's a fluke, a once-in-a-while happening.

When a positive talking mother sees her son hit a ball that helps his cricket team win their game, she later tells him,

'I'm so proud of you. You did really well, and all that cricket practice is really paying off. You did well in the last game too, and I bet you'll do even better in the next one. Your schoolwork is improving, you've been keeping your room tidy, and you've been eating fewer sweets. I'd say you're doing well in all kinds of ways.'

This is a classic universal, internal, permanent explanation.

A mother who's less aware of the importance of what she says to her children might say:

'Well, you were lucky that time. That bowler gave you a ball that no one could have missed. And it's a good thing the wind was blowing out towards left field. What a shame you don't bat more often. You'd better enjoy the glory while it lasts. You've got that science test tomorrow, and you know it's your worst subject.'

The powerless parent uses a specific, external, temporary description for the same event. The boy's sporting achievement is an isolated event, due to external factors, and certainly not something that will continue. Which parent do you suppose has the happier, more successful child?

In business, the most effective leaders are those who publicly credit members of their teams when they succeed. If you want to develop loyal workers who keep on getting better and better, make sure you give them credit for their achievements. The same is true of personal relationships — great friendships are built on mutual admiration. Think how much it means to you when someone you respect, trust, and perhaps love, gives you heartfelt recognition for your personal accomplishments.

In the chapters that follow, you'll meet people who benefit from taking credit for their own accomplishments. You'll also see the beneficial results of acknowledging the credit others deserve for their achievements. Be a positive talker; give credit where it's due.

12. *What's Your Excuse?*

You offer your colleague a lift home, and when you arrive she invites you in for a cup of coffee.

Say out loud to yourself:

'Oh, you'll have to excuse the mess. I left in a hurry this morning and the place looks terrible.'

Now say:

'Welcome to my home.'

Whose home will appear neater to you? Where will you feel more comfortable? Who sounds like the more confident, secure person?

What a good hypnotist can do with a group of otherwise serious, reserved business executives attending their company's annual dinner is utterly amazing – and hilarious. Gil Eagles is one of the world's finest. He's hired by IBM, AT&T, and other top companies when they want a world-class performance for their most important events. He can put a group of corporate leaders on stage, and within a few minutes, have them impersonating Elvis, reeling in huge imaginary fish, or behaving like demanding drill sergeants. Sitting in the audience, you just can't believe it when you see Joe, the mild-mannered, rather shy senior accountant you've known for years, up there clicking imaginary castanets and performing a spirited flamenco dance in front of a thousand employees.

Gil is quick to debunk the popular misconceptions about hypnotists. He does not put his subjects into a trance or induce a state of suspended consciousness. What any hypnotist really does is help his subjects create and live out a mental image.

If he suggests that they'll be embarrassed and look like fools, they won't co-operate. Instead, Gil brings his group of volunteers on stage and paints an elaborate and reassuring mental picture so they can see themselves succeeding. As they sit – eyes closed – in a row of chairs facing the audience, he tells them that they'll feel **relaxed** and emphasises that the whole purpose is **entertainment**. He says, '*You* will be the **stars**, and I will share the credit.' He asks the watching audience to 'Give these **brave** people a round of applause.'

With these statements, Gil creates a mental picture in his subjects' minds: they will be relaxed, brave and entertaining star performers. Then he helps them act out those images.

Gil's success as a hypnotist is based on a single premise: people act out the pictures in their head. After more than 4000 masterful performances, he's very conscious of the images he creates on stage. Off stage, we all unconsciously project images we really don't intend. Gil and I both learned something about creating unintended pictures when I visited him and his family.

After giving a speech in New York City, I phoned Gil and he offered to pick me up in Manhattan and drive me out to his home in New Jersey. From there, we'd head north to relax with his family at their weekend cottage in the Poconos. 'All right, I'll pick you up at 1 o'clock in front of the hotel. You'll have to excuse my car, it's a battered old Cadillac.'

Sure enough, he pulled up at the hotel in a marvellous classic Caddy and we drove to his home in Short Hills. His is a very exclusive, affluent community of company executives, doctors and lawyers. Many of the houses are million-dollar mansions. As we walked into Gil's large, beautiful, antique-filled home, he said, 'You'll have to excuse the mess; the dog has absolutely devastated the whole downstairs.'

Soon we were all seated in the roomy Cadillac, cruising north through Pennsylvania to enjoy a weekend at the Eagles' lakeside cottage. As we pulled into the drive, dozens of deer grazed along the roadside, the view over the small lake was serene, and their lovely house on the shore looked very inviting. Gil's welcoming comment was, 'You'll have to excuse our little shack.'

I've never enjoyed a more relaxing, comfortable weekend, or appreciated better friendship. There was absolutely no need for Gil to offer any excuses for anything. His home, car and cottage were all delightful.

Unintentionally, though, Gil had 'programmed' me to notice the slightly worn leather upholstery in his car and the teethmarks his magnificent Husky had left on the legs of the sofa.

When I brought this to his attention later, Gil couldn't believe he'd created those images. He's tremendously successful and is anything but insecure, yet he had unconsciously painted mental pictures that could make him appear ashamed of his home and car and cottage.

The first step in using more powerful language is to become conscious of your negative habits so that you catch yourself immediately after using a powerless phrase. Then you learn to catch yourself just *before* using the powerless version, and make the positive talking substitution. And finally, you develop the unconscious habit of speaking powerfully all the time.

If you're ever fortunate enough to visit Gil, I expect you'll now hear him saying, 'You can't miss me, I'll be driving a classic white Cadillac. You'll feel completely at home with my family. We're not stuffy or pretentious, as you'll see when you notice how comfortable our dog feels gnawing on the furniture. And you'll love our cosy cottage in the Poconos.'

When I'm on stage delivering a positive talking seminar, I often catch myself letting a powerless phrase slip out. I may say 'but' rather than 'and', or 'I'll have to check on that', rather than 'I'll be glad to check on that.' To my live audience, and to you, my reader, I emphasise the critical point: positive talking isn't a destination, it's a journey. Every day I'm aware of my language and working to improve it. You can do the same.

When you say, 'You'll have to excuse my . . . house / car / cooking', your apology has two effects. First, you draw attention to a condition **you're** uncomfortable about – and the other person may not otherwise have noticed. Second, you make yourself appear insecure.

Have you noticed that people who offer excuses rarely need to? As soon as they say, 'You'll have to excuse my messy house,' you're probably thinking, 'What's she apologising for? It's a lot neater than mine.' Or, 'She's right. Now that I'm looking, I can see that those ornaments need a good dusting.'

If people are going to be offended by the appearance of your home, or messy office, or dirty car, let them. It's their loss. In reality, most won't notice what you're uncomfortable about – if you don't draw attention to it. And those who do shouldn't concern you. If you've invited your boss to dinner and are genuinely concerned that your tiny flat or orange box furnishings will make a negative impression, meet at an appropriate restaurant instead.

In short, don't apologise for something you feel insecure about. Fix it or forget it. Given the choice of meeting someone who's insecure and uncomfortable – with good reason or not – and someone who seems content and happy, I'd much rather be with the relaxed person.

QUICK REFERENCE

What you can do right now:

Stop making excuses and apologising for some imagined shortcoming. Either change it or forget it.

Instead of saying,

'You'll have to excuse my messy flat. I just haven't had time to clean it up this week.'

Say,

'Come in. It's great to see you.'

Instead of saying,

'Sorry about the piles of junk in my office. I've been so busy lately, I'm afraid it looks a complete shambles!'

Say,

'Come into my office, I'll move some of these things out of the way.'

Instead of saying,

'We could take my car if you can put up with the old banger. I'm planning to get a new one – this one's going downhill fast.'

Say,

'Let's take my car.'

Instead of saying,

'You'll have to excuse my car/mess/hair/house.'

Say,

Nothing!

13. It's Just My Opinion

The executive whose phone you're answering is unavailable, and the caller asks when he should ring back.

Say out loud to yourself:

'I'm afraid I don't know. I'm only the receptionist. I could be wrong, but maybe in the morning. That's only a guess, I really can't say for sure.'

Now say:

'My name's Bob Wilkins, and I'm the receptionist. Please tell me what you're ringing about, and I'll arrange to have her secretary call you back.'

Which sounds like someone who takes pride in his work? Who has low self-esteem, represents his boss badly, and is unlikely to get very far in his career?

One of my clients asked me to participate in a panel interviewing two final candidates for a senior management position. Both possessed superb technical skills; each had demonstrated that they were more than capable of managing a similar department.

While other panellists asked specific questions about the candidates' experiences and career achievements, I concentrated on how each one spoke.

The first candidate began by saying:

'I'm Gwen Moss, and I'm here as a candidate to manage your Call Centre. Two days ago, I received my parcel of background information and the set of six formal questions you're asking each candidate. I'll begin by answering each of them for you.'

The second began by saying:

'I'm Brian Bayer. Unfortunately I only got your information and questions a couple of days ago, so I must confess that I haven't really had much of a chance to go through them in detail. I've had a guess at some of the questions and what I think you want to know. I could be way off. After all, it's only my opinion.'

One of the formal questions asked the candidates to 'Please describe your philosophy regarding customer service processes.' This question was broken down into important areas including recruiting staff, training them, measuring quality versus productivity, and so on.

The first candidate said,

'I firmly believe that . . .'

and she went on to explain some of her beliefs about customer service, including:

'Front-line employees must be able to solve problems, not pass the buck.'
'If you're in doubt – DON'T EMPLOY.'
'If you're not moving ahead, you're falling behind.'

The second said,

'I've done a little handout for you on my home computer. You'll have to excuse me, but I couldn't do it on a laser printer, so it doesn't look too good. Unfortunately I only have access to an old dot matrix printer. As you'll see I've included some of the things I like to say about customer service. They're just some of my little slogans.'

And they were listed in his handout:

'Service should be worth waiting for.'
'Motivate employees to welcome difficult callers.'
'Marketing is a philosophy, not a department.'

As the hour-long panel discussion concluded, each candidate was given a few minutes to summarise.

Gwen said:

'I feel ideally suited to manage this department, and I want to work with you. In the words of your CEO, which I read in your most recent annual report, "I can't think of a more exciting place to work". I can see why he said that. This is where I want to be. Thank you for your consideration.'

Brian said:

'Well, I don't have much to add at this point. It's really up to you now. I'm sure I'm just one of the people you're considering. I noticed your CEO said, "I can't think of a more exciting place to work." I thought that sounded good, and I'm only hoping I'll get the opportunity to work here.'

Aside from the candidates' phrasing, they were evenly matched. Both had very strong skills, backgrounds and technical competence.

The dramatic differences in their levels of self-esteem were evident in their speaking styles. The first candidate confidently presented her answers to each question. The second (who'd had the same amount of preparation time) apologised for not having had enough time to prepare more thoroughly. The first stated her analyses with conviction; the second excused his by characterising them as 'only my opinion'.

When it was time to summarise, the first, without being arrogant, presented herself as the ideal choice. The second lowered himself to 'just one of the people you're considering' when in fact he was one of the two finalists.

The substance of what each said carried equal weight. Their styles of saying it were polar opposites. Consider their two lists of customer service philosophies, for example. They could easily have been swapped; both made sense and summarised important principles. Prefacing Gwen's list with an 'I firmly believe' statement added importance to them. Prefacing Brian's with the denigrating phrase, 'They're just some of my little slogans,' devalued them.

My recommendation was to recruit the first candidate. What's yours?

Kay White is responsible for telemarketing training for a large company. She believes that our words reveal how we really feel about ourselves. They serve as a barometer that indicates our self-esteem levels. A poor self-image becomes a self-fulfilling prophecy. She says, 'How you're treated depends on the way you behave. If you say you're "only" a telesalesperson, you're saying you don't think much of your position, and customers treat you as someone with little authority.'

Kay teaches her trainees to avoid belittling language. They listen to each others' self-descriptive language and tell each other if they hear diminishing terms. Her 'coin-in-the-jar' technique is particularly effective. Rather than just keeping a stroke tally of their verbal slips, trainees actually deposit some money in the kitty each time they put themselves down. Each 'plink' reminds them to think about the value of self-supporting langauge.

Kay also recognises that her middle managers play an important role. They help shape an employee's self-image with every comment they make. She seeks to rid managers of such comments as,

> 'Considering your performance last month, I'm not at all surprised that you failed to reach your target this month. I can just never count on you, can I?'

You may react to those phrases by saying, 'But what manager would ever be so stupid (and cruel) as to say things like that?' Well, plenty do. Maybe you've worked for one.

One of Kay White's important goals is to show her managers how to commend and reprimand employees. When someone performs well, she reminds managers to avoid personality-oriented praise, and instead offer specific behaviour-oriented compliments.

Rather than saying:

'You're a real asset to my department, and I'm pleased to have you here,'

say specifically what you notice:

> **'Joanne, you did an excellent job of handling that customer's question. Your answer was accurate, and you gave it in a friendly way. Your word choice and tone of voice were both very supportive. I really appreciate your good work.'**

Kay reminds her managers that such praise must always be sincere. If it's not, the listener discounts what he hears, thinking to himself:

> 'I can tell when someone's trying to manipulate me. I know what you **really** think of me.'

The result of insincere praise is a counter-productive undermining of the employee's self-image. This low self-esteem then leaks out whenever the employee talks to customers.

When it's necessary to reprimand an employee, a manager's goal should be to change unacceptable behaviour, not diminish the person's self-image. Kay recommends using the 'criticism sandwich' technique. Sandwich the negative information between two positive messages:

> **'Terry, you've really improved your customer liaison. For example, your answer to that last caller's question was completely accurate. Your tone of voice could have been friendlier, and I'd like you to work on that in the next**

call. Keep up the good work with your accuracy. I can see that you've really mastered the technical aspects of your training course.'

Whether talking to yourself, describing your accomplishments, or commenting on another person's performance, avoid diminishing language.

QUICK REFERENCE

What you can do right now:

You're not 'just' or 'only' anything. Describe yourself, your beliefs and your accomplishments positively and proudly.
Instead of saying,

'I've only been here for a few months, but it seems to me that . . . .'

Say,

'I've been carefully observing for the last few months, and it seems to me that . . . .'

Instead of saying,

'Well, it's only my opinion, of course, and I could be wrong, but I would say . . . .'

Say,

'I believe . . . .'

Instead of saying,

'I'm just the receptionist, so I probably wouldn't be able to help you.'

Say,

'I'm the receptionist and I'll be happy to help you.'

Instead of saying,

'I'm only the . . . .'

Say,

'I am the . . . .'

14. *Is 'Luck' Getting the Credit for Your Hard Work?*

A project you initiated has just received significant recognition from your firm's parent company. Your boss tells you that you're being talked about at headquarters as someone to watch. 'How did you do it?' he asks.

Say out loud to yourself:

'Well, I'm not really sure. I suppose I was just lucky. I've handled dozens of similar projects and someone just happened to notice this one.'

Now say,

'I worked hard! On that particular project, I incorporated the feedback I'd received on my last report, and it really seemed to make a difference. I have an excellent support staff and they contributed a great deal too.'

Which sounds like the employee with the brighter future? Whose good work is likely to be repeated on the next big project?

If you don't get on well with your general practitioner, and you suddenly need a doctor, where do you turn? In many parts of America people can contact the successful referral service, Ask-A-Nurse. You can phone Ask-A-Nurse 24 hours a day, free of charge.

Let's say you wake up at 3 a.m. with a throbbing left

foot. There are no cuts or bruises – but it hurts so much you can hardly get out of bed. Should you try to sleep, then limp in to work and see if it feels better later? Soak it in warm water? Or see a doctor?

A call to Ask-A-Nurse puts you in touch with a friendly, professional registered nurse who asks you about your symptoms. She uses a computer program that prompts her to ask the appropriate questions, and follows strict medical procedure. As you answer, it becomes clear to her that you should be examined straight away.

The nurse directs you to emergencies at a nearby hospital, and warns them to expect you. After the visit she rings back to check that you were well cared for at the hospital. If you need to see an orthopaedic physician, or another specialist, she'll recommend a suitable one nearby. Of course, if all you need is an aspirin and a bandage until you can contact your own physician, she'll say so during your initial call.

Ask-A-Nurse is a terrific marketing and public relations tool. Not only does it bring in new patients, it also forms the basis of a long-term relationship between the hospital and the patient. The scheme also offers tremendous benefits for the community. Free of charge, anyone can receive a registered nurse's confidential, professional assessment. (Only physicians provide diagnoses.)

As you can imagine, the success of the scheme rests squarely on the shoulders – or voice – of the nurse who answers your call. Is she technically competent? Does she ask the right questions? Is she pleasant and understanding? Does she give the right answers? If she sounds vague, or seems unsure of her assessment, you're not likely to trust her advice.

Hospitals that use the Ask-A-Nurse service are very particular about whom they recruit. Interviews are extensive, and begin with telephone screening. After all, if the nurse can't handle the pressure of having a job interview over the phone, how will she cope when a frantic mother calls to say that her child is seriously ill?

When the manager asks an applicant about her strengths and weaknesses, she'd better not um and ah. Wrong answer:

'Oh well, I'm not really sure what my strongest points are. I suppose, um, well, it's hard to say. I was pretty lucky to get my last job at Bellevue Hospital in New York. You get everything thrown at you there, you know. So I suppose you could say I've been involved in a pretty wide range of situations.'

Right answer:

'My two greatest strengths are what make me feel confident about pursuing this opportunity with you. First, I really enjoy working with people in need. That's why I entered nursing in the first place. Being able to talk to and help 30 to 50 patients on the phone each day, compared with 15 or 25 in a ward, is very appealing. Second, my medical experience is wide-ranging. Early in my career I set my sights on working for the most diverse institution I could find, and that was Bellevue Hospital in Manhattan. We built an outstanding nursing team there, and I'm pleased to have played a major role in reorganising the department.'

In the words of Pat Stricker, Ask-A-Nurse manager at the Toledo Hospital in Ohio:

I like it when people aren't afraid to tell me what they're good at. If they say, "Well, um, I don't know," they probably lack the self-confidence we're looking for. On the other hand, if they're egotistical or boastful, I know they won't fit in well with the team.'

Life is like one long series of interviews. People are sizing you up constantly – before you've got the job, when you're being considered for promotion, at significant milestones, and during normal daily conversations. When you deserve credit, give it to yourself. People whose opinions can help you succeed want to believe in people who already believe in themselves.

There are two big reasons for giving yourself credit whenever you're proud of your own accomplishments:

(1) Others respect you for it, and (2) You deserve and benefit from it.

Don't write off your accomplishments as 'lucky'. People don't respect that kind of response. What you should really say is,

> 'Thank you. I worked hard and I'm very grateful for this recognition. My support team helped a great deal too.'

The way you react to praise helps others size you up as someone who is either boastful, falsely modest, or appropriately appreciative.

The second reason for accepting credit when you deserve it is even more important. We all respond to rewards, and those that carry the most weight may be the rewards we give ourselves. When you say to yourself,

> 'I feel so good about winning this award. I worked hard and this makes it worthwhile.'

you've reinforced your own successful behaviour.

In other words, giving yourself credit results in immediate and satisfying ego gratification, and it also encourages repeat performances.

When screening candidates during job interviews, I've noticed that their overuse of 'I' phrases is a real turn-off. When a candidate says,

> 'I accomplished this and that, I won such-and-such an award, I turned our department around, I was responsible for a 22 per cent increase in profit ...'

the interviewer may feel cautious about this person's ability to work well with a team, and may also question the individual's professed 100 per cent responsibility for departmental achievements. It's much more effective to share the credit without hogging it all yourself:

> 'Our department made some very significant improvements while I was manager. Together we increased our profits by 22 per cent, and as a result I was voted Manager of the Year.'

Take credit for your achievements. When others ask, let them know – modestly – that your success is a direct result of your hard work, plus the support of the others who helped. And when you talk to yourself, be sure that you reward and reinforce your own role in creating your successes.

QUICK REFERENCE

What you can do right now:

When you succeed, modestly acknowledge your own role in attaining your accomplishments, both to yourself and to others.

Instead of saying to yourself,

'Goodness, I can't understand why they picked me for this award. I haven't really done anything special to deserve it. I was just lucky.'

Say,

'I don't always give myself enough credit. This award is proof that my talents and hard work are appreciated by others. It's time I recognised more of my own accomplishments.'

Instead of saying,

'A lot of things just sort of went my way. I was lucky enough to guess right about the projection for next year, and it all came out more or less as management was hoping it would.'

Say,

'I drew on my past experience to do the projection for next year, and, having incorporated management's views, the results were very accurate.'

Instead of saying,

'I was lucky.'

Say,

'I planned well and worked hard.'

15. *What They Don't Know Won't Hurt Them*

While visiting friends, someone suggests that you play bridge. Mary asks if you'll be her partner.
Say out loud to yourself:

'Well, I'll be your partner, but I'm really not very good at cards. You'll have to forgive me if I do anything stupid. I hope I won't make us lose.'

Now say:

'Great, let's play.'

Which sounds as if Mary will regret having asked you to be her partner? Which leaves the door open for an enjoyable, challenging game?

There are so many situations where people 'cover themselves' by building a safety net of excuses, anticipating that they'll fail. The chances are that if you say nothing people won't realise you're insecure about your abilities. The only person being super-critical of your performance is . . . you.

Last summer I set myself a personal goal of joining in with three volleyball games. That may not seem like much of a goal to you, but for me it was important. I wasn't very athletic as a boy, and never voluntarily joined in any sporting events at school. As a result, I've felt insecure about participating in sport.

Still, there's no good reason why I shouldn't be a good athlete. I'm tall, well-proportioned and have reasonable coordination. My only shortcoming has been my attitude.

Sure enough, I did achieve my modest goal and joined in those three volleyball games. I enjoyed them thoroughly and played creditably. During the third game a brother and sister approached and asked if they could play. The sister, Sally, a young woman of about 25, joined our team. She walked on to the court and said, 'Oh, are you sure you want to have me on your team?' Sure enough, she missed most of the balls that came towards her, but her lack of skill was exceeded by her lack of self-esteem. Every time she missed the ball, she'd say, 'Oh, I'm sorry, I'm so bad at this. If you want me out of the team just say so.' It became embarrassing to play with her because we could all imagine how awful she was feeling, knowing that she'd probably miss the next ball.

Soon it was her turn to serve. She immediately prepared us all by saying, 'This is going to be terrible. I can never even get the ball over the net.' And of course she didn't. It was obvious that no one had ever shown Sally how to serve, so I called for a break and gave her a quick lesson. The other team, being good sports, gave her another chance. On her next try, Sally made an excellent serve which the opposing team did not return. Twice more she served very well, gaining points each time.

I could identify with Sally because I know that every time I've been coerced into some kind of athletic encounter, I've begun by apologising for my expected poor performance and repeatedly told myself off for playing badly. Sally would have been much better off – as would I – had we simply played our best. None of the other players were experts, and her lack of skill would hardly have been noticed had she not kept drawing attention to it. Her performance would have been much better if, instead of deriding her own serving ability, she had simply said, 'Would one of you show me how to hold the ball when I serve? It's been a while.'

Do your best without telling people that you think your best isn't very good.

QUICK REFERENCE

What you can do right now:

You're probably far more critical of yourself than anybody else is. Just go ahead and enjoy doing as well as you can.

Instead of saying,

'Well, I'm certainly no artist, but I'll try to do a rough sketch to show how this new process would work. I hope you'll be able to see what I mean despite all the horrible scribble.'

Say,

'I'll draw a diagram of this new process to make it clearer.'

Instead of saying,

'I'm terrible in the kitchen, but, well, I did my best. I tried to make Fettucine Alfredo. I hope you can force it down without feeling too sick.'

Say,

'I hope you'll enjoy eating the Fettucine Alfredo as much as I enjoyed cooking it.'

Instead of saying,

'I'm really not very good at this.'

Simply do your best without excuses.

16. *Catch People Doing Things Right!*

You're talking to a colleague about your department's tidy appearance. He comments that your area always appears well looked after – much neater than his own.
Say out loud to yourself:

'Well, that's the way I like it. I'm always telling my staff that I expect our offices to look shipshape. They do pretty well. They'd better.'

Now say:

'You know, you're right. My staff really are good about keeping this area looking nice. Do you mind if I tell them you said so? I'd like them to know that I'm not the only one who appreciates their good work.'

Which sounds like the manager whose staff will continue to keep the area neat and put in a little extra effort? Which one probably has a morale problem, high turnover and employees who don't really enjoy working for him?

While on holiday with my family, I had my first encounter with a professional wrestler. Hawk, a member of the Road Warriors professional wrestling team, stayed in the same holiday complex. Within hours of his arrival at the resort, every child and most of the adults staying in the complex knew he was there. He was immense and muscular and certainly caught everyone's attention the first time he stretched out beside the pool in his leopard-patterned swimming trunks.

Having observed a steady stream of autograph-seekers and picture-takers approach him by the pool, I settled into a deckchair beside Hawk's and began to read. I probably wouldn't have chosen to sit so close to him, but it was one of the few chairs available. There was a kind of 'clear-zone' around Hawk. I suppose most people felt as self-conscious as I did about sitting there and attempting not to stare.

It was impossible to ignore the conversations he was having, considering his very loud, gravelly voice. It was understandable that very few adults approached Hawk to talk, because he certainly had an imposing physical appearance. Many children, however, walked straight up to him and conversed quite comfortably. Most were young boys, and I imagine that many had probably said to their parents, 'One day I'd like to be a big, strong muscleman like him.'

I was surprised to hear what Hawk said to these children. He spoke in entirely positive terms. He didn't tell the boys, 'You're a little pipsqueak, but if you work really hard, maybe one day you'll be big and strong like me.' Instead he told them that they were already growing strong. Even when skinny, under-developed kids came up to ask for his autograph, he'd find something positive and complimentary to say. 'Your arms are really long. I bet you're a terrific basketball player.'

After overhearing many such conversations, I got up the courage to start talking to him myself. I told Hawk how impressed I had been by the way he handled the children, and it was then that I realised he was doing so totally by design. He said, 'It's so easy to do, and it can make such a difference to these little kids.' Not only was there a heck of a nice person underneath all the flesh and muscle, he was consciously guiding those children to think highly of themselves.

Hawk was genuinely moved when I complimented him on his positive behaviour with the kids. I'm sure he hears no end of praise and admiration for his physique, but I suspect that very few people stop to tell him they admire anything deeper than his physical appearance.

That conversation completely changed my view of professional wrestlers. I've never before intentionally watched a professional wrestling match on television. If all those other big fighters are as sensitive, caring and positive as Hawk, I may yet become a fan.

Ken Blanchard and Spencer Johnson were right! When they took the business book world by storm with *One Minute Manager* and its many spin-off books, they advocated 'Catching People Doing Things Right'. They correctly asserted that this was one of the most under-used and effective management tools around.

Positive talkers give credit wherever it's due, especially when it's unexpected. This whole book emphasises two major audiences for your language: you, and the other people who hear you. Everyone benefits when you give others credit for their accomplishments, even when it's just something little.

I live in a lovely wooded area near Seattle. The approach to my street is a long, steep hill with a central flower bed that extends for nearly a quarter of a mile. Throughout the year, the plants are trimmed, pruned and rotated. After the azaleas' brief glory of intense, fiery red blossoms, somebody plants pansies in great numbers. When they wither, marigolds and lobelias appear. Somebody goes to a lot of trouble to keep that flower bed looking good. It's not automatic. The 'somebody' is Susan. Every now and then I've noticed this woman digging and clipping and pruning and planting.

I'm sure most of my neighbours have thought to themselves how beautiful and well-tended that flower bed is. One day I thought it was time Susan found out how much her work is appreciated. I pulled over to the kerb as I drove down the hill, lowered my window, and said,

'You do a wonderful job. I often see you out here, making sure the plants look good. Your effort really pays off; they always look great. Thank you for being so conscientious about your work. I enjoy seeing it every time I drive up or down the hill.'

Her face blossomed as beautifully as any of the annuals she had been planting. With a big smile, she said,

'I'm really glad you enjoy my work. I like doing it too. Thank you for stopping. It makes me feel really good to know that you notice.'

She's not the only one who felt good. Offering someone a compliment can make the complimenter feel almost as good as the one who's complimented. With Susan the gardener, that moment of seeing her smile and feel appreciated was well worth pulling over for. And, what's more, I feel extra good every time I drive past her handiwork, knowing that she probably thinks about my comment from time to time. When I see another round of fresh flowers coming into bloom, I know I haven't taken them or her for granted.

Since much of my speaking and consulting work is dedicated to fostering professionalism on the telephone, I'm especially attentive to people who do a great job handling my phone calls. When a secretary answers the phone in a clear, friendly manner, I take a moment to comment. When a customer service representative deals with my question professionally, I let that person know he's done a good job. I especially enjoy complimenting switchboard operators who handle my calls well. Hotel switchboard operators, in particular, seem amazed that a guest should take an extra moment to offer a commendation. I end up feeling just as good as they do.

Invest a moment, every day, to 'catch people doing things right', as Ken and Spencer suggested. Tell them what you notice and why you appreciate it. You'll both feel great about it.

QUICK REFERENCE

What you can do right now:

Go out of your way to compliment people and give them credit for doing things right, especially when they don't expect it.

Instead of saying to yourself,

'Someone really does a nice job with the lettering on those signs at the chemist. It must be someone who studied calligraphy.'

Say to the shop manager,

'Who makes those signs I see all over your shop? They do a really good job, and I'd like to tell them so myself.'

Instead of saying,

'Her children are so quiet and well-behaved.'

Say,

'You've obviously given your children a lot of positive attention. They talk to everyone so politely and intelligently.'

Instead of saying,

'My daughter is a big help around the house.'

Say,

'Darling, you are a big help around the house, and I appreciate it.'

17. *You're About as Old as You Say You Are*

Your adult children invite you to join them for the annual camping trip.

Say out loud to yourself:

'I'm not a kid any more, you know. I'm too old to enjoy that kind of thing.'

Now say:

'That would be fun. I'd enjoy a change of scene, and of course I like to be with you.'

Which sounds like someone who'll live out his years in happiness, surrounded by people who enjoy his company? Which is likely to become a bitter, depressed, lonely old man his children won't really want to visit?

An audience member asked Dr Norman Vincent Peale, author of *The Power of Positive Thinking*, why, at age 92, he continued to give speeches rather than quietly retiring to enjoy life.

'Why? ... I'll ... tell you ... why. Because, ... despite all the speeches ... I've given ... over the years, ... and despite ... the many books, ... there are still a few negative thinkers out there!'

The audience rose and applauded in unison.

As a member of the National Speakers Association, I've had the opportunity to meet, hear and work with many of the world's most celebrated speakers. At the Association's 1990 Awards Dinner, my wife and I sat with Dr and Mrs Peale. This isn't normally a celebrity-hungry group, but the members really went mad about Dr Peale.

After dinner Dr Peale was called on to the stage so he could announce that his friend and one of our colleagues, Michael Frank, had been selected to receive the Council of Peers Award of Excellence, the highest award given for speaking skills and professionalism. As Dr Peale's name was announced, all 1500 tuxedoed and bejewelled professional speakers rose and applauded.

After his presentation, another speaker and I carefully helped the venerable gentleman down off the platform. As the audience continued applauding, the nonagenarian turned to us and said with a chuckle, 'You look like you're practising to be pallbearers!' It was the only reference I heard him make to his age that whole evening, and he certainly meant it jokingly.

Later I asked Dr Peale for his prescription for enjoying life at such an advanced age. He said simply, 'Live your life and forget your age.'

Many people spoil their happiness by talking about how old they are. Hitting their fortieth birthday seems to trigger a stream of 'I'm getting old' exclamations that continues for the next 40 or so years. Why do many celebrities conceal or falsify their ages, as if acknowledging their years would reduce the esteem in which their fans hold them? It's not a person's chronological age that matters, it's his attitude toward ageing that makes all the difference.

My dictionary defines 'youthful' as 'Having accomplished or undergone little erosion.' Losing youthfulness is a process of erosion, and we do much of it to ourselves. We wear away our own self-images by commenting disparagingly on our advancing age. We send supposedly funny birthday cards that deride our friends as they mark the anniversaries of their birth. The collective effect of all these comments is to erode our feelings of youthfulness.

Just as there's no point in hastening your own erosion, why contribute to anyone else's feeling of 'getting too old'? I recommend boycotting the greeting cards that make disparaging jokes about ageing. Although meant in jest, they merely contribute to a collective consciousness that sees ageing as a negative condition. Even if they're hard to find, scan the greeting card shelves and look for cards that help buoy up your friends and relatives as they get on in years.

QUICK REFERENCE

What you can do right now:

Use neutral or positive phrases in reference to advancing age. Don't erode vitality by speaking negatively about again.

Instead of saying,

'I'm going downhill, my hair's going grey, my wrinkles are showing, I'm just an old bag!'

Say,

'I keep fit and I look good.'

Instead of saying,

'At my age, you know it's very hard to have fun. My body is starting to fall apart.'

Say,

'At my age, I enjoy different sorts of things. What did you have in mind?'

Instead of saying,

'I feel worse and worse. I'm getting too old.'

Say,

'I feel good.'

III. *REBOUND RESILIENTLY*

POSITIVE talkers rebound resiliently. Of course they experience setbacks, and they bounce back again. They learn from their experiences and emerge stronger than they were before. Have you ever noticed how many very wealthy people have been completely broke or even bankrupt at some stage in the course of accumulating their wealth? They didn't give up. They learned, and rebounded resiliently.

In Section II, I discussed Dr Martin Seligman's research on the 'explanatory styles' and language characteristics of optimists and pessimists. There, we examined how positive talkers describe *positive* events. When things go *badly*, the positive talker uses the opposite explanatory style. He concentrates on specific, external and temporary explanations. The *powerless* talker sees problems as being universal ('Not only is this situation going badly, but everything in my life is awful'), internal ('It's all my fault'), and permanent ('Things never go my way, and this is just another example that proves it').

As a positive talker, when you experience negative situations in life – when you lose a job, or you don't get a promotion, or your child has a difficult time at school – you consciously replace universal, internal and permanent explanations with those that are specific, external and temporary. When a positive talker doesn't get promoted, he says,

'I missed out on that promotion, and I understand why. I haven't yet mastered the new software, and it's really vital that I learn to use it well. I know I can, once I've been through the training course. I've done well in my career in the past, and I'm sure there are more successes in store for me. I'm certainly glad I'm doing so well in other areas of my life. My health is superb, I have a wonderful family, and I have excellent job skills. I know I'm ready to advance in my career and I'm going to start working towards that next big jump.'

It's entirely natural to respond negatively, when things go wrong; I often do it myself. Don't expect positive talking principles to come naturally. Work at them.

In the following chapters you're going to meet people who have rebounded from disastrous situations. They've changed bankruptcies, personal failures, alcoholism, depression and smaller setbacks into positive experiences. You may be confronted with a variety of setbacks today, yourself. When they occur, use the positive phrases in the next few chapters and you'll come out ahead.

18. *Does Your History Repeat Itself?*

You lose your job. You're two payments behind on your mortgage. Your wife walks out.

Say out loud to yourself:

'I know why this is happening to me: I'm a failure.'

Now say:

'I know there's an important lesson in all this. What can I learn?'

Which sounds like the person who will never recover from these setbacks? Which is the winner who will learn valuable lessons and emerge wiser and stronger?

How would you feel if, at age 40, after 20 years of business success, you had to call your father and ask him to lend you £300 . . . so you could afford to file for personal bankruptcy?

In the mid-1970s, Michael McCafferty left his position as a successful salesman at IBM in order to start his own business. He did very well with the Philadelphia-based computer service he founded, and ran it profitably for seven years. It was acquired by a larger firm, and the director of the new parent company offered Michael an agreement that would make him a very rich man.

But then the director died, and Michael realised his agreement had never been put in writing. The new director decided not to honour the verbal agreement and Michael was cheated out of his promised stock.

Humiliated, he packed up and left for Chicago, where he successfully ran another service bureau three times larger and 'cashed out' after two years. Chicago's winters were too cold for him, so Michael, in his mid-30s, headed for San Diego, bought a house on the beach and a vintage Ferrari, and lived a wonderful, carefree life. It got boring. That's when an old business associate approached him about starting a new venture.

Michael was intrigued. He coupled his mastery of computers with a recognition that people will always want convenient access to more information. He created the first Electronic Yellow Pages system and perfected the technology that is still the basis for a growing industry.

Then his partner got cold feet and pulled out. Michael had no doubt that the business would be a big success and decided to invest further, on his own. He sold the Ferrari and bought a battered 1972 Chevrolet. Then he gave up his house on the beach. And before long, all the money he had was invested in the failing business.

While Michael was reeking of desperation, a shark caught his scent. A fast-talking moneyman offered to rescue the company and get Michael back on his feet . . . in return for a 51 per cent share of the company. Other partners were brought in and Michael's business crumbled.

Michael McCafferty stopped working and sank into a deep depression. He had no income and lived off his credit cards. Bankruptcy was the only way out, but he couldn't afford the court filing charge! So his dad bailed him out one last time.

For a full year Michael repeatedly said to himself,

'Why me? What happened to my money, my Ferrari, my carefree early retirement? How did that fast-talking moneyman end up with everything?'

His all-consuming thought was, 'Why did this happen to me?' After a year of destitution, desperation and depression, the answer dawned on him: 'Because I let it.' It was that simple. The world hadn't victimised him; he had invited his misfortune. He had trusted the wrong people, he'd behaved naively, he hadn't got important agreements in writing, and he'd given up authority.

He had conceded control. Not just financial ownership of the company, but control of his fate too. He gave up control of everything by thinking that things 'simply happened to him'.

Once he realised what the lesson was, he got to work. He read Og Mandino's classic, *The Greatest Salesman in the World*, and wrote out its affirmations on a card:

'Today I begin a new life.
I will persist until I succeed.
I will live this day as if it is my last.
I will act now.'

He read them aloud first thing in the morning, last thing at night, and several times during the day.

Michael looked back on his 'failures' and drew lessons from them. He distilled them into 'The Ten Commandments for Managing a Young Growing Business', and he made a commitment to obey them. On St Patrick's Day 1983 he founded a new company and named it Remote Control (of course). As I write, Michael's company has grown at an average annual rate of 133 per cent over the last seven years. Based on the lessons he learned from his multiple 'failures', he created the best-selling software package in its category, 'TeleMagic'. It helps hundreds of thousands of sales professionals around the world become more organised, more profitable, and maintain control. Finally Michael McCafferty is the multi-millionaire he deserves to be.

Positive talkers consciously recognise that failing is a vital part of succeeding. When they say 'I failed!' it has an exclamation mark after it, and is closely followed by, 'And here's what I learned.' Losers just say, 'I failed.' It's followed by a full stop. As America's famous football coach, Vince Lombardi, said,

'It's not whether you get knocked down. It's whether you get up again.'

Michael McCafferty got up again and drew invaluable lessons from his mistakes.

Don't fear failures, welcome them. May you have many, and learn important lessons from them all.

QUICK REFERENCE

What you can do right now:

When you're confronted with a 'failure', look for the lessons you can learn.

Instead of saying,

'What a stupid thing to do. How could I have scraped together my entire life savings and invested it in property, only to discover that the market was falling flat? I'm a complete failure.'

Say,

'Putting all my eggs in one basket hasn't paid off, and this investment has not produced an acceptable profit. I've learned some valuable lessons, though, and I won't take an uninformed risk like that again.'

Instead of saying,

'That's the fourth job interview I've had and again they didn't even phone me back or send a letter. I must be a failure.'

Say,

'My approach to these job interviews hasn't been working. I've learned that the interviewers don't tend to phone back. Maybe that means I should take the initiative. After the next one, I'm going to wait a few days and then ring to ask if I'm still being considered for the job.'

Instead of saying,

'I failed.'

Say,

'Here's what I learned . . . .'

19. *Half-Empty, or Half-Full?*

You've been working closely with an influential director in your organisation for the last five years. Your current project is critically important to your future, and the director has been your mentor, and prime supporter. She calls you into her office and announces that she's accepted another position with a leading organisation in your field.

Say out loud to yourself:

'Now what will I do? She believes in me and fully supports me on this project, but she's leaving. Now I'm high and dry. I'll have to start all over again with someone new. This is a major setback.'

Now say:

'Now that she's leaving, I'll keep in touch with her as a good contact outside our company. And I'll be able to develop a strong new relationship with her replacement. This is an interesting change.'

Which sounds like the person who's going to feel depressed and go into a career 'holding pattern'? Who's going to dive in eagerly and capitalise on a new set of circumstances?

In the publishing world, an author's most important contact is the commissioning editor. This is the person who believes in the writer and supports the project right from the start. The editor negotiates the author's advance payment and many other critical elements of the contract. Once the publishing company has made a commitment to produce the book, the author relies on the editor as the internal spokesperson; the editor liaises with the publicity, promotion and sales staff to maximise sales of the book.

The editor who championed my first book, *Phone Power*, also initiated this one. With the *Say What You Mean* manuscript half-finished, she phoned to tell me she had accepted a position with another publisher.

My immediate reaction was:

'That may be a great career move for her, but what a setback for me! Now I'll have to start all over again and work with an editor I've never even met. Maybe that person won't even like my book. What if she abandons it and lets the sales force ignore it?'

You know the old saying about the glass: it's either half-empy or half-full, depending how you look at it. I was looking at my glass and seeing nothing but risks and problems.

I hope you don't think that positive talking comes easily or automatically for me or for anyone else. It requires constant concerted attention and effort. Five minutes after hearing this 'bad news', I got up from my computer keyboard, walked to the window of my study and, looking out at the stream and woods, forced myself to say,

'What great news! Now I'll have a strong advocate at another publishing house. When I meet my new editor, I'll be able to "sell" the book to her so she's full of enthusiasm right from the start. Instead of presenting a half-baked idea, I can show her exactly what the book's about. And, with her fresh perspective, she'll probably have plenty of new promotional ideas.'

As I look back now, I can see that my editor's departure opened up many new opportunities for me. The glass was half-full − and filling.

When confronted with any situation that represents a change from what we're accustomed to and relying on, most of us naturally see the negative side first. I often do it myself. The trick is to recognise that seeing the negative 'half-empty' aspect first doesn't mean that's the only way you can, or will, look at it.

Seeing that the glass is half-full is a learned skill. Don't feel discouraged if it doesn't come immediately or naturally. Do use the power of your language to turn things around.

Be on the lookout. Whenever 'This is bad news because . . . .' crops up in your comments to yourself or others, stop and replace that line of thought with, 'This is good news because . . . .' You can't exploit opportunities if you don't see them. Train yourself to see the good side by using a fill-the-blanks technique. Force yourself to complete the sentence: 'There's a good side to this situation, and it's what I choose to focus on. This is great news because . . . .'

QUICK REFERENCE

What can you do right now:

Rephrase negative reactions to unexpected changes and say, 'This is great news. It means that . . . ,' and then start looking for the positive result that can follow.

Instead of saying,

'I didn't get the promotion I wanted; that's terrible news.'

Say,

'I didn't get the promotion I wanted, and that's good news because it means I can broaden my horizons. I'm going to make a few phone calls and see what my talents are worth to some other companies. Then I'll have a better idea of whether or not I should stay here.'

Instead of saying,

'Damn, the sale of our house fell through. Now we have to start all over again.'

Say,

'OK, that buyer backed out. I'm glad it happened now instead of at the last minute. This means we can reassess the market and be sure we've priced our property to make the most of the present situation.'

Instead of saying,

'The car repairs won't be completed by lunchtime, as the garage promised. That mucks up my whole schedule.'

Say,

'Since the car won't be ready by lunchtime, I'm going to take this opportunity to walk over to the library down the road from the garage. I haven't been there for ages. It's a good thing my plans have changed.'

Instead of saying,

'I see some very negative consequences resulting from this turn of events.'

Say,

'I see some very positive consequences resulting from this turn of events.'

20. *If Only I Had . . .*

You attend your trade association's annual convention and, on reading the programme carefully, realise that tomorrow night's awards dinner is a black tie event. Your dinner jacket is hanging in the wardrobe at home.

Say out loud to yourself:

'If only I had read the programme more carefully before I packed. Why don't I ever plan ahead for these things? I'm going to look completely out of place.'

Now say:

'I'll check with the hotel receptionist and ask about renting a dinner jacket. Next time I'll be sure to read the programme carefully several days before the convention.'

Which sounds like the person who's bound to have a miserable time at the awards dinner and may well repeat the experience next year?

A coronary bypass operation can really make you stop and think. For a friend of mine, it also prompted a host of 'If only I had . . .' regrets. In his early 40s, this young man had concentrated on his career, given his family far too little attention, and ignored all advice about sensible nutrition.

From his hospital bed, Jerry kept talking about his regrets: 'If only I had spent more time with the children.' 'If only I had avoided all those high-cholesterol foods.' 'If only I had led a more balanced life.'

To hear him talk, you'd have thought he was writing his own epitaph. Despite the successful surgery, Jerry was still wishing for what might have been, rather than concentrating on mending his ways and aiming for an improved quality of life.

Jerry's recovery began when he stopped saying 'If only I had . . . .' He agreed to delete this phrase from his vocabulary, and his family and friends helped reinforce the point by interrupting whenever he started to say, 'If only I had . . . .' Soon Jerry was saying, 'I haven't enjoyed my family as much as I deserve, and I'm changing that, starting now.' 'I haven't been sensible about my eating habits, and I'm now changing to a healthy, nutritious diet.' 'I've been out of balance, and now I'm consciously working towards a balanced life.'

Today Jerry is like a new man. It wasn't just the operation that did it. His verbal surgery played an important role too. You don't need a doctor's help to begin surgically removing your own 'If only I had . . .' regrets.

When you hear someone using the phrase 'If only I had . . .' you can usually be sure that he's stuck in the past. He's floundering in regrets, preoccupied with what can't be changed. The appropriate time to talk about a regrettable past is when you're conducting a retrospective analysis of what went wrong so you can change it.

On my travels I've occasionally had my checked-in luggage lost or delayed and once even went on stage wearing tennis shoes and jeans. When that happened, I wished I had taken my luggage on board with me. I've also carried my bulging suitcase as hand luggage, dragged it from gate B–1 to gate E–32 while running to catch a connecting flight, and wished that I had carried on nothing but my briefcase. In each case it would have been easy to get bogged down in 'If only I had . . .' thinking.

Rather than dwelling on the past and regretting my actions, I've used these experiences to focus on the future: 'When I pack and check-in all my business clothing, I risk losing it; when I carry it on, I'm weighed down. So, starting now, I will find a better answer.' My solution has been to check in all my luggage, including the clean suit I plan to wear on stage. I fly wearing another suit that I could use for my presentation if my bags are lost.

If a salesperson just misses winning the regional sales contest, you can easily assess her chances of triumphing in the future based on the way she describes her loss. If she says, 'If only I had sold 5 per cent more, I could have won. What terrible luck,' her prospects are poor. If she says, 'I was just 5 per cent short of winning, and I'm sure I can be 5 per cent more effective by assessing my potential customers more carefully. Next time I'll be more productive,' you're hearing a winner.

The same 'If only I had . . .' phrasing is common to managers, negotiators and other professionals who consistently fall short of their potential. In fact almost anyone who says 'If only I had . . .' is probably holding himself back from greater success in his chosen endeavour.

Help yourself eliminate negative, regret-filled thinking by doing away with the phrase 'If only I had . . . .' Replace it with a positive, forward-looking statement like 'Starting now, I will . . . .'

QUICK REFERENCE

What you can do right now:

Focus your attention – and your language – on what you will do to shape your future positively. Don't dwell on the past by talking about what might have been.

Instead of saying,

'If only I had held on to my Volkswagen for a few more years, I could have sold it for a lot of money as a classic.'

Say,

'Next time I buy a car that might appeal to collectors I'll check investment prospects before I sell it.'

Instead of saying,

'Maybe we could have had a family if only I had been more open to the idea before my wife had to have a hysterectomy. Now it's too late.'

Say,

'I'd still like to have a family. We can contact some adoption agencies or find out about becoming foster parents.'

Instead of saying,

'If only I had.'

Say,

'Starting now, I will.'

21. *Bottoming Out*

Your life is going downhill. First you are demoted, then you start drinking, then your marriage crumbles.
Say out loud to yourself:

'I shouldn't have to go through this. I know things should be better, I just don't know where or how to start.'

Now say:

'I will change my life. I will start making things better today, right now. Nobody else will do it. I will take action.'

Which sounds like the person who will wait and wait for something to happen, and then wonder why it never does? Who will start taking action and begin moving in the right direction?

For 'Tom', it all boils down to a single truth:

'You can act yourself into right thinking, but you can't think yourself into right action.'

When you hit bottom, you can't think your way out of it. You must **do something**. And for Tom, the most effective action was to change his language.

I met Tom while I lived in Venice Beach, California. On the surface Venice looks like an arty, chic community. Film producers and famous artists move there to be offbeat.

There's another side to Venice. Hippies who never quite moved out of the 60s live in old shacks and drive psychedelically painted cars. They coexist with a violent community of hard drug-users. It was there that Tom hit bottom. He was unemployed, broke, living in a slum, stumbling along to the next bottle of wine, the next pill. He didn't realise he was an alcoholic until he had completely collapsed physically and emotionally.

Tom's life began to change when he met an Alcoholics Anonymous member who dragged him along to his first meeting. Judging by outward appearances, Tom was indisputably a loser when he began the 12 steps of recovery advocated by AA.

His new sober friends gave him support and faith. They encouraged him to adopt an attitude of positive expectancy. They told him to visualise what he wanted his life to be like, and he did. He concentrated on seeing himself as a successful, sober person. He wasn't sure *how* he would become successful; he just had faith that the way would become clear if he concentrated on the end rather that the means.

Then Tom's liver failed. Admitted to St John's Hospital in Santa Monica, he lay in bed and reflected. He knew he wanted to be successful, he held an attitude of positive expectancy, he was thinking himself towards his goal, but he wasn't seeing any results. Looking back now, Tom views his stay in hospital as a blessing. He had the time − sober − to really examine his feelings. He concluded that there was a saboteur at work inside him. He'd visualise a goal, and then his lifetime of angry feelings would take over and prevent him from reaching it.

So, he began to **do**, not just think. He began writing out his affirmations:

'I, Tom, dare to be prosperous.'
'I, Tom, relentlessly visualise success in every endeavour – and I act to make it so.'
'I, Tom, reject thoughts of failure.'
'Failure will never overtake me if my desire to succeed is strong enough, and I act on that desire.'

There in the hospital he began repeating them to himself, over and over again. Soon after his release Tom got a job. A new friend who was a very good salesman encouraged him to pursue a career in sales, so Tom went to work for a small company that sold computer printer ribbons by phone. He applied himself, took action, and – one day at a time – became the top salesman.

Tom eventually left to start his own company.

Still repeating his affirmations, he lay on Venice Beach and visualised a room with 40 people, all producing profitable sales, all working for him. He started small, making the sales calls himself from his small flat.

Today Tom is director of a company that manufactures top-quality computer products in its 30,000-square-foot factory and employs 130 people. Tom has a talented, loving, supportive wife (whom he met through AA), a young son, and a balanced life. When work pressures increase, he rewards himself by taking his family to a remote part of Idaho, where they own a rustic log cabin originally hand-built by a famous film star. As Tom says, 'It's not where you start, it's where you finish.'

Tom's story isn't unique. Tens of thousands live lives as rich as his, and have rebounded from circumstances as dismal as his too. They all have one thing in common: They didn't just decide to change their lives – they took action.

If you are at a low point in your life, take action. Begin by saying – not just thinking – what you want to be true. Use the power of affirmations and spoken words to move yourself towards the success you deserve. Lao-Tzu didn't remind us to think about taking steps, he simply wrote:

'A journey of a thousand miles begins with one step.'

QUICK REFERENCE

What you can do right now:

When you're at a low point, write out your affirmations, using positive language, and say them aloud to yourself. Don't just think, act.

Instead of saying,

'I tend towards failure. Look what a mess I've made of my life already.'

Say,

'Failure will never overtake me if my desire to succeed is strong enough, and I act upon it.'

Instead of saying,

'I'm visualising myself as a successful person, putting my troubles behind me. But nothing is changing.'

Say,

'Today I am taking action. I am moving towards the success I deserve.'

Instead of thinking to yourself,

'I'm a loser.'

Say,

'I am a winner.'

22. *Bouncing Back*

You're managing a department that's threatened with extensive cuts in personnel. Just when your workers need strong emotional support and effective representation, they discover that their union official has skipped off to Barbados with most of the union funds. A workers' committee asks to have a meeting with you to discuss what the future holds.

Say out loud to yourself:

'I don't know what to say. The situation looks bad, and I don't see how things are going to get any better.'

Now say:

'**I understand how uncertain you must all be feeling, and I know we're facing big challenges. We've overcome difficulties before, and we'll get through this present situation too. We are a good team, and we will bounce back. I know we'll be able to come up with a good plan by working together.**'

Which sounds like the manager whose team will get busy and start thinking of solutions? Which is about to face a worsening situation with morale declining and productivity sinking?

At 3 p.m. on a Friday afternoon, the furniture removers arrived with empty cardboard boxes. The locksmith walked toward the vice-president's office and began changing the lock. Word spread quickly.

Barbara Grego was the telemarketing manager for House of Almonds, then a wholly owned subsidiary of Tenneco. Under her management, her department had grown from four people to 27 in a single season. The company had discovered that salespeople could phone corporate gift buyers and secure very profitable orders for almond gift packs. They weren't selling nuts so much as convenience. Companies that traditionally sent gifts to their customers could avoid all the shopping, gift wrapping and postage by turning to House of Almonds. They'd send or fax their customer address lists, indicate which ones should get which category of present, jot down what the gift tags should say, and House of Almonds would take it from there.

The prime selling season spanned just a few months, from August to November. The pressure was intense during this period; tension and stress plagued the department. Facing some critical challenges over internal funding, and undergoing the normal growing pains any department would experience during a 500 per cent expansion, Barbara called me in as a consultant to advise her on management issues and train her rapidly growing telemarketing team. One of the telemarketing department's prime assets within the organisation was a vice-president who believed in Barbara's management. Then, at the peak of the crisis, he was given the sack.

As her mentor's office was cleared out, Barbara's reaction was to plaster the word 'Buoyant' throughout the department. She pinned posters to the walls and had key rings made for every employee. They all said just one word: 'Buoyant'.

Barbara Grego wanted to remind her staff – and herself – that they were buoyant. Life has its ups and downs, and if there were no challenges or upsets, it would be very dull.

Positive talkers recognise that during the tough times they grow stronger. Circumstances may seem to conspire and push us briefly underwater from time to time. When they do, it's easy to feel as if we're drowning. The important thing is to remember that adversity tests our mettle, giving us an opportunity to surface again, stronger and wiser.

The bleakest circumstances often precede a promising change of events. It's crucial to picture yourself, and the team you lead – whether that's your family or a work group – getting your heads back above water. Picturing it isn't enough. Talk about it. Let the words you use reflect your determination to stick it out with the expectation that things will improve.

QUICK REFERENCE

What you can do right now:

When you hear yourself describing a setback as a terminal disaster, rephrase your description to recognise that you will bounce back and move on.

Instead of saying,

'My department's been slashed, my boss has been fired, and my career's going into a nosedive.'

Say,

> 'I'm buoyant enough to surface from this turbulent situation. Experiences like these are what strengthen my talents as a manager.'

Instead of saying,

> 'Since my best friend moved, I feel at a loss. I just don't see how I'll ever get over this loneliness.'

Say,

> 'I really miss Nicole since she moved. Now I'm going to phone Judy and start getting to know her. I know I'll make new friends.'

Instead of saying,

> 'I've damaged the tendons in my foot and the doctor says I'll never play again.'

Say,

> 'I'm going to really take care of myself so my foot will heal quickly. Then I'll find a sport that won't be so hard on my feet.'

Instead of saying,

> 'I'm going under.'

Say,

> 'I'm going to bounce back.'

23. *It's Over!*

You've just returned home from a two-week holiday. Unlocking the front door, you find that your burglar alarm has been switched off. You're sure you set it before leaving and fear that someone may have broken in while you were away.

Say out loud to yourself:

'Oh no! What if we've been burgled? They've probably stolen my jewellery! And what if they've taken the computer with all my records on the hard disk? I'll be in a real jam. What am I going to do?'

Now say:

'We may have been burgled, so let's carefully check all through the house. If valuables are missing, the insurance will pay for most of them. Let's do a thorough inventory.'

Who's the best candidate for an ulcer? Which person would you rather be with when a real emergency occurs?

Stew Leonard approached the woman at the airport's Hertz car rental counter and asked, 'Have you seen a giant yellow chicken?' The rental agent laughed and said, 'No, as a matter of fact, I haven't.' So Stew asked, 'Which way to the escalator?' The rental agent replied, 'Escalator? There's no escalator at this airport.'

Stew Leonard founded and built the world's largest dairy store. Tom Peters made him famous all over the world when he extolled Stew's brand of customer service in his 'Excellence' books and video. Tom Peters said, 'I've searched the world over looking for excellence in every nook and cranny. One of the best examples I found was a dairy store in Norwalk, Connecticut . . . Stew Leonard's.'

Stew had been invited as the keynote speaker at a conference on quality presented by Frank Perdue of Perdue Chicken. Frank holds an annual conference with notable guest speakers and invites his most important customers, suppliers and key staff members to attend. This particular conference was being held at Amelia Island, an exclusive resort off the coast of Florida near Jacksonville.

In confirming the arrangements, Frank had said, 'Stew, don't worry about a thing. As soon as you step off the plane, I'll have someone in a giant yellow chicken costume waiting by the escalator to meet you. The chicken will escort you straight to the limousine. The island is connected to the mainland by a bridge and it's only an hour's drive from the Jacksonville airport.'

But when Stew stepped off his plane, there was no chicken waiting to greet him. So he proceeded to the baggage reclaim area. After watching all the other passengers claim their bags and leave, the carousel came to a stop, and Stew thought, 'No chicken, and now no luggage! My clothes, my slides, my notes, everything I need is in my suitcase.'

He finally decided to rent a car on his own, head out to the island, and make arrangements to find his lost luggage later. When he asked the Hertz agent how long the drive would take, she told him it would take several hours. 'Several hours? But Frank Perdue told me the island was less than an hour away from Jacksonville!' She replied, 'That's true, but we're not in Jacksonville, Florida. This is Savannah, Georgia!'

Stew suddenly realised that he had left his flight to Jacksonville prematurely, at the intermediate stop. His luggage had gone, along with the plane, to Jacksonville.

Stew paused for a minute and considered the situation. Within the hour his plane would be landing in Jacksonville without him; the passengers would stream off and notice a man in a chicken costume in the arrival area. The limousine driver would be faithfully waiting at the bottom of the escalator as Stew's unclaimed luggage went round and round on the carousel.

Stew followed his own prescription for dealing with setbacks. He laughed for a moment and said to himself, 'It's over!' There was no point in dwelling on the situation; it would not help at all to get cross with himself for having left the plane too soon. Instead he used his time and energy to contact Frank Perdue to make sure someone picked up his luggage in Jacksonville. He then made his way directly to the island on a chartered aeroplane.

As Stew told me the story, he said: 'My policy is that whenever there's absolutely nothing to be gained by dwelling on the stupidity of a situation, whenever something really bad happens and it seems like all my plans are ruined, I just say to myself "It's over." That's my secret for making the best of the situation. In this way I save my energy to make things better. As it turned out, the plane I chartered got me to the island in plenty of time. My bags were delivered to the hotel, I had a great new story to add to my talk, and the conference was a success.'

Stew Leonard's advice reminds me of the most helpful book I read at high school. It was Dale Carnegie's classic, *How to Stop Worrying and Start Living*. In it he suggests a simple three-step process for ending fears and worries. It goes like this:

1. Identify exactly what it is that you're worried about and answer this question: what is the very worst thing that could happen as a result of this situation?

2. Accept 'the worst' as if it were a reality. Imagine that it has already occurred. Having now accepted your worst fears, there is no need to expend any of your energy worrying about having them come true. They have come true!

3. Now redirect the energy that you had been using to worry about your worst fears coming true, and instead, do something useful that will help prevent them materialising.

I've used that simple formula in a wide range of situations and have found that it never fails. Let's put it to the test in Stew's predicament.

1. **What's the very worst that could happen?** Well, Stew could have found that there were no chartered flights available and realised that it was impossible for him to reach the island in time to give his talk. He could have missed it altogether and disappointed his friend Frank Perdue. The audience would also have been disappointed. Stew would not have been able to accept his professional speaking fee for the engagement and might well have suffered some financial penalty. He would have returned home knowing that he had disappointed his friend and his audience. If that had happened, Frank would probably have seen the humorous side of the situation, entertained the audience himself, and

the conference would have gone ahead with an altered programme.

2. **Accept 'the worst' as if it were true.** In his mind's eye, Stew would visualise Frank Perdue walking on stage the following morning and announcing to the audience that Stew had left the flight one stop too soon and wouldn't be able to give his talk. They would have muttered in disappointment and probably laughed a bit. Although unlikely, Stew might also have had a phone call from Frank berating him for missing the engagement.

Would Stew be in physical pain? No. Would his career be threatened? No. Would his future be ruined? Of course not.

He would have disappointed his friend and the audience and suffered a financial loss. That's all. Accepting this, Stew would still want to carry on – and leave this mistake in the past.

3. **Now use the energy that you might have fretted away and do something constructive.** This is exactly what Stew did. He got on the phone, made the chartered flight arrangements, notified Frank, and everything turned out fine.

In this situation the complexities of the back-up arrangements were such that a few minutes' delay could have made all the difference. The chartered aircraft might not have been available a short while later. The pilot could have gone home for the day. The small, unlit airport at Stew's island destination might have shut down for the night. Had Stew paced round the airport bemoaning his situation and berating himself for making a stupid mistake, the 'worst that could happen' might well have actually happened.

Think of how many times you've seen people drain their energy by constantly rehashing the details of a negative situation they're in. This cannot make things any better, and may well make them a lot worse. At the very least, the worrying and moaning makes everyone involved feel lousy. When you're in a predicament, accept circumstances as they are and use your energy to move in a positive direction.

QUICK REFERENCE

What you can do right now:

When things seem to be heading for a disastrous outcome, stop and ask yourself, 'What's the very worst that could happen?' Accept that eventuality as if it were true and say, 'That's all; it's over.' Then, get to work applying your energy to create a more positive outcome.

Instead of saying,

'It looks as if I won't be able to finish the report on time, and I'm dreading having to face my boss if it's not done. I can just imagine what he's going to do if I don't finish on time.'

Say,

'I may not be able to complete the report on time. The worst that could happen is that the boss will be disappointed and ask me to stay late to finish it. He's not going to fire me, he'll just be upset. That's all; it's over. Now I'll start summarising the remaining sections of the report so I have a good outline to show him.'

Instead of saying,

'What rotten luck! I cut my hand just before the netball championships. Now I can't play and my team will probably lose. It'll be all my fault.'

Say,

'With this cut on my hand, playing netball is out of the question. I'm the best shooter on the team and without me, we may lose. That's all. As I can't play, I'm going to coach Anne so she'll improve her shooting.'

Instead of saying,

'This is terrible, and it could get a lot worse.'

Say,

'Even if the worst happened, I could live with it. So there's no point worrying. That's all; it's over. Now I'm going to start making things better.'

IV. *ACCEPT RESPONSIBILITY*

POSITIVE talkers eagerly accept personal responsibility. Rather than blaming others, they see themselves as being in control of their own fate. They're not victims and they don't talk as if they're casualties of circumstances beyond their control.

Positive talkers shape their circumstances. When they're not good, they get busy and change them. When it is truly not possible to change a situation, the positive talker actively manages his reaction to it.

In the next few chapters, you'll meet people who guide their own fates. They apply positive language to very significant situations, like a crippling motorbike accident, and to seemingly insignificant situations, like being 'too busy' to relax with a good book. You're about to see how positive talkers show others – and themselves – that they are responsible.

24. *Watch Where You Point That Thing!*

You're training a new employee who seems to have excellent potential. However he still seems confused about a few of the office procedures you've already explained several times.

Say out loud to yourself:

'You make me so frustrated! I've explained this job over and over again, and you just can't seem to get it right.'

Now say:

'I feel frustrated when we don't understand each other. Which areas shall I explain a little more clearly?'

Which statement is more likely to encourage cooperation? Which will result in changes that improve the situation?

My mother, Edith, was full of homespun wisdom. In my mind's eye, I can see her smiling and pointing. As a teenager, when I made an excuse for not completing my homework on time, she'd extend the index finger of her right hand, curl back the other three fingers, and point at my imaginary excuse. If I said I couldn't complete a book review because my typewriter was jammed, she'd break into her radiant smile and, with a twinkle in her eye, emphatically point at the poor old Smith-Corona and wiggle her other three fingers. This was her way of reminding me that my attention should be concentrated on those other three fingers because they were pointing back at *me*. The index finger identified only the object of *imagined* responsibility.

Her pointing motion made me rephrase my description of the predicament. Instead of saying,

'The typewriter is jammed, and I can't use it, so I can't finish my review in time.'

I'd look at the other three fingers and remember to redirect my attention back to myself, and my role, by saying:

'I didn't plan ahead and check the typewriter. As it's jammed, I'll hand-write my review tonight and get the typewriter fixed tomorrow.'

Salespeople tend to grumble about customers who don't buy:

'That cheapskate can't see past the purchase price. He can't even understand that in the long run our equipment is less expensive to own and operate and will serve him better.'

Where's that salesman's index finger pointing? At the customer. When he redirects his attention to the other three fingers, the scenario changes:

'I still haven't convinced my customer that the long-term operating costs are a more important consideration than the price. I'll use another approach and make it clearer.'

If he stays focused on his index finger, there's not much else he can do but look for another customer. He discards the first non-buyer after declaring him defective. What he's really saying is:

'If that customer can't see beyond the purchase price, it's his own fault. He's not clever enough and doesn't deserve to be my customer anyway!'

Paying attention to the other three fingers is much more productive. We can't really change our customers. We can alter our own behaviour. If we set out to change others, we're likely to become more and more frustrated and disgusted about short-sighted customers. When we concentrate on changing ourselves, we improve our own sales techniques and become more and more effective.

The old finger-pointing routine is especially relevant in emotionally charged situations:

'You're driving me mad.'

Really? The other person is forcing you, against your will, to lose control and go insane?

I've taught many seminars for customer service professionals who deal with a steady stream of emotional callers. It's tempting for them to say,

'Those rude callers make me so angry! They raise their voices, they swear, and they imply that I've mucked up their accounts, even though I had nothing to do with it. They make me furious.'

The reality is, some callers do raise their voices, swear, and make inaccurate accusations. But they don't drive anybody mad. Mad people drive themselves mad by reacting to stimuli. It's not the other person's fault.

Redirecting attention to where the other three fingers are pointing – to yourself – changes the situation:

'When callers raise their voices and say certain words, I become upset. I need to depersonalise those situations. Certain words and actions trigger those reactions in me. I'm going to work on managing my reactions when I face those conditions in the future.'

When you meet someone who's superb at handling people who are upset, notice how they concentrate on their own reactions to stimuli. They're paying attention to the other three fingers. Emotional confrontations result not so much from what other people do as from how we react to them.

Whether your goal is to manage your own emotions or communicate an important idea to a student, employee or customer, focus on the three fingers that are pointing back at yourself. Changing the person or situation your index finger is pointing at is much more difficult and frustrating. You can always modify your own behaviour.

QUICK REFERENCE

What you can do right now:

Be on the alert for that pointing finger! Whenever you hear (or see) yourself directing blame or responsibility elsewhere, focus on the three fingers that point back at you.

Instead of saying,

'He just doesn't seem to understand.'

Say,

'I haven't yet made it clear.'

Instead of saying,

'These customers just can't get it through their heads that our price increase is reasonable and justified.'

Say,

'I need to do a better job of explaining why we've had to increase our prices.'

Instead of saying,

'You upset me when . . . .'

Say,

'I feel upset when . . . .'

25. *Use the Time You Have*

Your boss asks if you saw the article about your leading competitor in an industry trade journal. You've been working very hard on an important research project and have fallen far behind on your reading.

Say out loud to yourself:

'No, I didn't see it. In fact, I never have enough time to do any reading when I'm working on a big project. I just can't seem to get through all my work and I'm constantly getting more and more behind. I don't know what I'm going to do.'

Now say:

'No, I haven't scheduled time to read industry journals since I've been concentrating on the research project. I'd like to talk to you about our priorities and make sure

that I'm scheduling my time in accordance with your expectations.'

Which sounds like someone who's in control of his time? Who is flailing about, using time inefficiently?

It doesn't take a time management expert to verify that you have available 1440 minutes every day and 525,600 minutes each year. How you use that time is purely a matter of choice. Some people are phenomenally productive and continually accomplish the many ambitious goals they set for themselves. Others achieve very little and, when asked why, say, 'There just isn't enough time.'

When you say, 'There isn't enough time,' or, 'I just haven't had the time,' what you're really saying is that it's out of your control. You could accomplish more if you were given a few extra hours each day, but you haven't been granted that extra ration, so you can't get everything done. It's not your fault, you're a victim of time shortage!

Positive talkers accept responsibility for what they do accomplish, and for what they don't. Your achievements are a reflection of your choices about how you use time. Don't blame a failure to reach your goals on a lack of time.

I once shared a speaking platform with a medical doctor who specialises in treating over-stressed business people. We were both addressing a conference of sales and marketing executives. The people in that audience were definitely stressed. They create advertising campaigns, work towards their bosses' (often unrealistic) sales goals, and implement and administer sales targets.

In his 45-minute presentation, the doctor revealed that there's only one effective way to handle stress. Actually, he used 44 minutes to tell entertaining stories and one minute to tell us his stress cure-all:

'I'm often called on to present a full-day seminar on stress management. Sometimes, though, the group has a tight schedule, so I can also cover it in a half-day version. If a client's budget is limited, I can do a two-hour seminar. Even a one-hour keynote speech is no problem. I've been

studying and treating stress for many years and I have no doubt that I've found the answer. Since we have just a few minutes before my presentation ends, would you like to hear the ultra-condensed version? In fact, would you like to know the one-sentence, surefire, cure-all technique that never fails to cure stress-related syndromes? If you want to have less stress in your life, lower your expectations. *That's it.* That's all there is to it.'

As blasphemous as this prescription sounded to his audience of high achievers, he confirmed that it was the only one that really works. Destructive stress results from having unrealistic expectations. If we would all match what we want to accomplish with what we're realistically able to do, we'd be under much less stress.

Don't wish for more time. Take responsibility for how you use the time you have available, and recognise that what you do and don't accomplish is a reflection of the choices you make. Remind yourself of that by talking about your time in terms that acknowledge your role in managing it.

QUICK REFERENCE

What you can do right now:

Stop using phrases that suggest time is out of your control – that there's not enough of it. Acknowledge your personal responsibility with your language.

Instead of saying,

'I just haven't had enough time to finish it. I'm trying to get to it, but I just haven't been able to. I need more time.'

Say,

'I haven't finished it yet. I'm working according to priorities, and that particular task is something I've put on my list for next week.'

Instead of saying,

'This job is driving me mad! They expect me to get twice as much done as I can possibly hope to accomplish. I can't say no when they give me a new project or they'll think I'm not really dedicated. Meanwhile I'm really on the point of collapse.'

Say,

'I work better when I'm not feeling so stressed. My boss may not even realise how hard I'm working. I'm going to make a list of the projects I'm working on and ask him for some help in setting priorities. I'll explain what I can realistically accomplish and suggest that the lower priority items be assigned to someone else.'

Instead of saying,

'I just can't catch up; I don't have enough time.'

Say,

'I can catch up by managing my time and eliminating low-priority projects.'

26. *It's Not What Happens to You, It's What You Do About It*

You're working on an important project and the deadline is tomorrow. One key element isn't ready, and the project may not be finished in time.

Say out loud to yourself:

'It's not my fault.'

Now say:

'It's my responsibility.'

Which statement sounds like it's coming from someone who will take charge of his situation and make the best of it? Which comes from someone who's going to sit around blaming others for the situation he's in and do little to change it?

I'd never shaken a fingerless hand until I met W Mitchell. I first saw this unusual person at a National Speakers Association convention. I felt uncomfortable as soon as I noticed him across the hotel lobby. Confined to a wheelchair and grossly disfigured with extensive burns and scars, he was the kind of person who, because of his appearance, many of us choose to avoid.

When I saw him again, months later, at another convention, I still couldn't summon up the courage to approach 'Mitchell', as he likes to be called. I consider myself a friendly, outgoing person, but just kept thinking how awkward I'd feel reaching out for his scarred hand. Thankfully, he wheeled over and shook mine. I now know one of the most extraordinary people on this planet.

In the early seventies, Mitchell's motorbike collided with a laundry van in the middle of a busy intersection. Passers-by gasped as the motorbike petrol tank burst open and Mitchell became a human fireball. Today the only parts of his face that aren't scarred are thin strips of skin that were protected by his helmet strap.

After reconstructive surgery that included numerous grafts on to the stumps of his burned-off fingers and extensive physical therapy (not to mention months of excruciating pain), Mitchell bounced back. He qualified for his multi-engine pilot's licence; co-founded a highly successful metal-casting company employing over 400 people; ran for Congress; met US Presidents and Cabinet members; served as Mayor and enjoyed an active social life.

Then, while taking some friends up for a sightseeing flight, the small plane he was piloting crashed. As a result, Mitchell's burned, scarred, disfigured body was now also paralysed from the waist down.

You'd think he would have just given up after this second disaster. Instead he's gone on to become an extremely successful professional speaker. Mitchell wheels himself on to the stages of America's biggest sales meetings and conventions. He has appeared on national television and has been featured in *Time* and *Newsweek*.

Mitchell is cheerful and productive, travels the world, manages extensive property investments, and has a positive impact on a great many lives. How can he lead such a healthy life when he has so many handicaps, or 'problems'?

'I have no problems,' Mitchell says. 'That's a foolish word. I do have many instances where unusual, challenging circumstances confront me. I am fully responsible for my present situation. Sure, the laundry truck driver was legally liable for the accident – and I'm responsible. I don't mean I'm guilty, or at fault. I am responsible – able to respond.'

Mitchell sheds a whole new light on the concept of 'blame'. Many of us fall far short of achieving our true potential, and we often blame others. Can you think of friends who blame their parents, the educational system, a dishonest business partner, or a multitude of other reasons for their situation? Do you do the same?

Positive talkers acknowledge that they are responsible. When we blame others, we weaken ourselves. Instead of improving our situation, we step backwards. Other people and circumstances aren't what hold most of us back. *We* hold *ourselves* back because of the way we react to them.

Accepting responsibility means taking control of your life and the language you use to describe it. As Mitchell says, 'It's not what happens to you, it's what you do about it.'

QUICK REFERENCE

What you can do right now:

Accept personal responsibility for your present situation and decide to move forward rather than wasting energy by blaming your current condition on past circumstances.

Instead of saying,

'My parents couldn't afford to send me to university like yours did, so I wasn't lucky enough to get a degree. I had to go out and work while you were enjoying yourself at college. Nobody will give me a really good job. I can't help it.'

Say,

'I haven't been to college yet, and I have gained a great deal of practical experience in my various jobs. I plan to take evening classes and work towards a degree starting this summer. Meanwhile I'm looking into job opportunities for which my diverse practical experience will be an advantage.'

Instead of saying,

'I couldn't meet my sales target this month because my car broke down and I just couldn't get to many appointments. It was in the garage for a whole week. It's not my fault. I couldn't help it.'

Say,

'I had unexpected car trouble this week, so I used the time to phone all my long-standing customers whom I haven't talked to for a while. In the long run, I believe this effort will pay off. In the short run, it means I did not get to enough appointments to meet my sales targets this month.'

Instead of saying,

'I can't help it; it's someone else's fault.'

Say,

'It's my responsibility to change things.'

27. *You Can Count on Me*

It's Saturday morning and you're working in the paint department of a large home-improvements centre. A customer phones because his electric garage-door opener isn't working.

Say out loud to yourself:

'Sorry, I can't help you. The hardware department won't be open until 10 a.m. You'll have to ring back later.'

Now say:

'The hardware department will be open at 10 a.m. I'll be happy to help by taking down the details and passing them on. What is your name, please?'

Which sounds like the more responsive, helpful organisation? As a customer, which would you rather encounter?

By the eighth ring, I felt impatient. This hotel chain had a reputation for outstanding service, so I was annoyed when the operator at one of their hotels took so long to answer. Finally, after the eleventh ring, an operator answered and transferred me to reservations. I heard some clicking, and there was silence. I had been cut off!

I called again, waited nine rings, asked for reservations, heard the clicks and . . . damn!

The third time, my call was answered quickly. Rather than reservations I asked for the hotel manager. The operator placed me on hold while she paged him. After leaving me on 'silent hold' a little more than a minute, she came back on the line to tell me he was unavailable. So I said she could transfer me to reservations. You guessed it. Click.

You've no doubt experienced similar frustrations yourself. Since writing *Phone Power*, I'm on the alert for examples of excellent, as well as poor, handling of phone calls. I often count the rings and time the holds.

On my **fourth** attempt, the operator did connect me with the manager. He listened attentively as I described my experience. When I told him that I wanted to reserve a room for my family, and was afraid that I would be cut off if I were transferred again, he said,

'Mr Walther, I'm not going to transfer you. I will handle your reservation myself. Then I'll investigate the phone system and find out why you've been getting cut off. When will you be arriving?'

The manager could have transferred me, and hoped I would be connected smoothly. He could have offered to take my name and number and have someone ring me back to take my reservation. But instead he took responsibility and did it himself.

In his best-seller, *Swim With the Sharks Without Being Eaten Alive*, Harvey Mackay identifies many of the phrases that he's used throughout his incredibly successful career. When I interviewed him for this book, he said,

'There's a place in this world for anyone who will say, "I will take care of it".'

When you deal with people who say, 'I will take care of it myself,' you know that they are taking personal responsibility for the outcome. That doesn't mean they'll do the tasks themselves, it means they'll be accountable. The hotel manager didn't walk over to the computer terminal and type in my reservation. He did personally ensure that it would be handled properly.

QUICK REFERENCE

What you can do right now:

Even though you may not be the person who will actually perform the tasks, accept personal accountability when you offer to help someone.

Instead of saying,

'I can't help you with that, you'll have to talk to the customer service department.'

Say,

'Customer service are the best people to help with that question, and I'll stay on the line while I transfer you.'

Instead of saying,

'Only the regional director can authorise a change in policy. You'll have to phone her yourself.'

Say,

'The regional director has authority in the policy area you're asking about. I'll be glad to give you her direct number so you can discuss it with her yourself.'

Instead of saying,

'That's not my area. You'll have to get someone else to help you.'

Say,

'I'll help you myself by getting your message through to the right department.'

28. *Do You Choose to Lose?*

You work in a job that's well below your capabilities. You want to spend time with your family at weekends, and you don't want to drag a bulging briefcase home each night. A friend asks why you haven't actively sought to advance your career.

Say out loud to yourself:

'I just haven't been able to, what with the family and everything. I could be doing a much more responsible job, but unfortunately someone has to look after the kids at weekends. Mary doesn't get out much during the week, and she insists on playing tennis every single Saturday. I really don't have much choice.'

Now say:

'I've chosen to dedicate myself to my family at the moment. I'll concentrate more on my career three or four years from now. There will always be plenty of job opportunities, and now is the only time I can spend with my kids while they're small. I like giving Mary some

freedom at weekends. She certainly works hard during
the week while I'm at the office.'

Who's happy? Who thinks of himself as a victim of
circumstances?

One of the worst holidays I've ever endured was a two-week
stay in paradise with my family. The resorts were luxurious,
the weather was perfect, the beach was ideal. How could it
have been so miserable?

My wife has two children from her first marriage, both
teenagers. They usually live with their dad and they spend
some of their holidays with us, so I'm a part-time stepfather.
For this trip, we invited each of my stepchildren to bring one
of their teenage friends along for two weeks. In addition
to the four teenagers, we took our three-month-old baby,
Kelcie, who had not yet reached the 'sleep-all-night' stage
in her development.

The result was that for those two weeks I slept badly
every night. Then I woke up each morning and spent the
day reminding the four teenagers to close the refrigerator
door after taking out their food, to turn off the lights before
they went to bed, and so on. Rarely did they heed my
words.

As time went on, I became more and more irritable
and, in the end, blurted out to my wife that I had never
experienced a worse two-week period in my life. I blamed
the four teenagers for ruining our trip. The truth is that
those four kids behaved perfectly normally for thirteen- and
fourteen-year-olds. Kelcie is a terrific baby and slept as well
as you would expect any three-month-old infant to. Those
four teenagers and a baby did not ruin my holiday. I ruined
my holiday.

One challenge I face in writing this book is living up
to my own advice. Whenever I complained to my wife
about how the kids were wrecking the trip and making
me miserable, she reminded me that the decision to enjoy
or detest our holiday was completely in my hands. I 'chose'
to have a bad time. She got even less sleep than I did and

was equally inconvenienced by the kids' messiness and lack of consideration. Julie, though, chose to have a good time, and she did.

The children's behaviour was completely predictable. Before planning the trip, I could have anticipated what it would be like. When I started feeling resentful, I could have said to myself,

'Four teenagers are not going to think about turning off lights and cleaning their rooms. Our baby will probably wake us up a couple of times every night. I'm going to take those circumstances into account and choose to have a good holiday with my family.'

Since I didn't choose to have a good time, the bad time I did have was also my own choice and my responsibility.

One consistent characteristic of winners is that they claim responsibility for their circumstances. They don't play the 'victim'. They don't only claim credit and accept responsibility when things go well. They also embrace the concept of personal responsibility when things aren't perfect. That way they reserve the power to change them.

Powerlessness, the inability to change what you don't like, is a terrible feeling. Ask anyone who's been held as a hostage or prisoner.

Actually, there's very little that we can't change. OK, so you won't be able to alter the course of a tornado that's bearing down on your home. Those truly unchangeable circumstances, though, are relatively rare.

'There are two big forces at work, external and internal. We have very little control over external forces such as tornados, earthquakes, floods, disasters, illness and pain. What really matters is the internal force. How do I respond to those disasters? Over that I have complete control.'

LEO BUSCAGLIA
(Best-selling author and American authority on love and interpersonal relationships)

Winners see the distinction. We've all heard the old prayer:

'God grant me the serenity to accept the things I cannot change, change the things I cannot accept, and the wisdom to know the difference.'

The key is knowing the difference. Most things are in fact changeable. And our reactions to the few things that truly can't be changed are, in themselves, matters of choice. I could not change my baby's sleeping patterns, and could not 'control' those teenagers and instantly change them into gracious little adults. I could have changed my reaction to the circumstances. I could have **chosen** to enjoy myself despite the kids' behaviour.

Recognise that most of what you like and don't like in your life is changeable. And even with the few things that you can't change, you can choose to react positively or negatively. Take responsibility, acknowledge your choices, and use the word **choose** when you describe the situations you're in.

QUICK REFERENCE

What you can do right now:

Avoid 'victim' language; acknowledge your responsibility by using the word 'choose'. When you're dissatisfied with the way things are, choose to change them.

Instead of saying.

'I hate my job, but there's really nothing I can do about it. I'm stuck in this dead-end position, working for a boss I don't really like or respect.'

Say,

'For now, I've chosen job security rather than professional challenge. I could work with more inspiring people, and one day I will. I'm going to start improving my professional skills and looking into other opportunities. Meanwhile I'm glad I've created a secure position for myself here.'

Instead of saying,

'I'd love to buy a new car, but we can't afford one. I know it's embarrassing to drive this old banger, but there's just nothing we can do about it.'

Say,

'Yes, I'd like a new car, and one day we'll have one. At present, though, we're making a choice to keep the old one so we can afford to have holidays and go out for dinner whenever we want to.'

Instead of saying,

'I can't change things, I didn't get myself into this fix.'

Say,

'I choose to make the best of this situation.'

V.   *ENCOURAGE COOPERATION AND REDUCE CONFLICT*

ZIG ZIGLAR says:

'I believe that you can get everything in life you want if you will just help enough other people get what they want.'

Positive talkers are masters at working **with** other people and helping them get what they want. The most successful people are those who ensure that their 'partners' also do well.

Positive talkers use their language to encourage cooperation and defuse potential conflict. They use 'win-win' phrasing and form partnerships with others. Their aim is to ensure that both sides in all negotiations win – that there isn't a loser.

One of my clients is a very successful developer who has acquired major properties around the country and developed them into profitable holiday flats and time-share projects. Today Mark is the marketing director for a beautiful resort in Wisconsin. Not only has he had a very successful career himself, he's also guided a whole team of telephone professionals to work towards impressive mutual success.

When I asked him what techniques he uses, I heard a lot of positive talking phrases. He explained that every member of his team starts the year by writing out his or her personal goals, which are reviewed with managers each week. Some new employees have a tendency to write, 'Here's what I hope to do,' or 'Wouldn't it be great if . . .' Mark made it very clear that employee's goals are always rewritten to use the positive expectation language of 'I will achieve . . .'

He also pointed out that the goals don't just relate to individuals, they pertain to the organisation as a whole, as in, 'This is what we will accomplish together.' Using positive, conflict-reducing language, is more effective than if he were to gather his employees together and say, 'Here's what you have to do to make my resort a success.'

In the following chapters you'll meet people who have succeeded in selling ideas and generating cooperation among others, who are good at stimulating group creativity, and who are extraordinarily successful at getting others to do what they want them to do. We are all 'salespeople' every day. We 'sell' our ideas to others and encourage them to agree.

You'll also learn the techniques employed effectively by talented 'peacemakers' whose area of expertise is calming people who have already become upset and hostile. Positive talking leads to increased cooperation and decreased conflict. If you need to work with other people, you'll find these techniques very helpful.

29. *Get That 'But' Out of Your Mouth!*

Your daughter has just passed an introductory diploma in computer programming. She's working towards a promotion at her company.

Say out loud to yourself:

'You did a good job, Suzanne, **but** you'll need to do more to be ready for that promotion you want.'

Now say this:

'You did a good job, Suzanne, *and* you'll need to do more to be ready for that promotion you want.'

Which sounds more encouraging? Which statement will stimulate Suzanne to continue pursuing her goal?

Every property market has its ups and downs, including California's. In the 1980s, Southern California seemed blessed with prosperity. My friend Peter Schweizer and I both invested in Californian properties throughout the '80s.

In 1990 Peter came up north to visit me in Seattle. As we walked in the woods, talking about our 'California days', he reflected on our properties, saying,

'Yeah, my holiday flat at Mammoth was a good investment, but it's so far away from Los Angeles; I just don't use it much. You sold your Venice Beach apartment building for a good price, but if you'd only waited another two years, you could've sold it for even more.'

Peter still owns his very comfortable holiday flat at an exclusive Calfornian ski resort. He bought it in the early 1980s for less than $20,000. He skis there five or six times a year, often lends it to friends, and also rents it out. His investment has paid off superbly, and he could easily sell it for many times the original purchase price.

Yet, as we talked, Peter's concentration was on the negative aspect: 'but it's too far away'. His attention was focused on the phrase following 'but'.

I am delighted to live in Seattle and I'm glad I moved away from Los Angeles when I did. My property investments in Washington have performed particularly well. Yet, again, Peter's focus was on the negative. The phrase following 'but' got the emphasis:

'but . . . you could've sold it for even more.'

I may have got a better price by selling my Californian property two years later. However I wouldn't have been able to buy in Washington just before the prices started going up there.

The effect of the word 'but' is to put two viewpoints in opposition to each other and to devalue one of them.

'It was a good investment, **but** . . . .'

makes you wonder if it was such a good investment after all.

'You sold at a good price, **but** . . . .'

takes away the compliment I was beginning to feel. In the first half of the sentence, my mind heard,

'You did well, George. You have a good sense of timing and anticipated the market well.'

As soon as '**but**' came out, I stepped back and heard,

'Well, maybe you weren't **that** astute. If you'd only waited a while, you'd have been much cleverer.'

Peter and I sat down on a rock overlooking the Seattle skyline and I explained that a simple substitution of one word makes a tremendous difference to the impact his statements have on others, and on himself.

'Yeah, my holiday flat at Mammoth was a good investment, *and* it's so far away from Los Angeles that I don't use it much. You sold your apartment building for a very good price, *and* if you'd waited another two years, you might have sold it for even more.'

This way Peter gives himself credit for his good investment sense while recognising that things have changed. He's no longer interested in driving five hours to his holiday flat. Both conditions, the holiday flat being a good investment, **and** his unwillingness to travel five hours to use it, coexist at the same time.

He's also complimenting me on selling my property at a good price **and** acknowledging that the selling price might have been higher had I waited.

The mere substitution of 'and' for 'but' reduces conflict by suggesting that two ideas can exist at the same time without one overruling the other. Peter's original statement has a much more positive, powerful impact when he uses 'and' rather than 'but'.

Sometimes 'but' is what you really mean.

'It's a very expensive house, but there's no view, the rooms are small, and the local school has a terrible reputation.'

Most of the time, though, we say 'but' out of habit, when 'and' would be a much better choice. Unless you really want to devalue the prior thought ('It's expensive, but bad value') you're better off substituting the conflict-reducing 'and'.

When I conduct training courses for sales professionals, one subject that's often requested is objection handling. For example, 'What can I do when the customer says, "But your price is too high"? The first step is to rephrase and repeat the customer's objection using 'and' rather than 'but'.

One of my first sales training clients was Xerox. Their business products division sells copier paper, toner and other supplies. It's common for customers to point out that they can buy paper much less expensively if it doesn't carry the Xerox name. New salespeople instinctively say,

'Our paper may seem more expensive **but** ...?'

As soon as a salesperson utters the word 'but', the customer 'hears' him trying to contradict her belief and she stops listening. People don't like to be told they're wrong. They immediately start to resist.

So, instead, I trained the salespeople to agree with their customers:

'Yes, our paper seems more expensive, *and* the cost of making copies includes much more than the paper itself. Cheaper paper, for example, has a tendency to curl and jam in the machine. That means your staff have to spend time clearing paper jams rather than dealing with important projects that increase overall profit.'

The customer isn't being told she's wrong; she's simply being provided with more complete information on which to base her buying decisions.

Replacing 'but' with 'and' creates a more cooperative atmosphere in sales situations, negotiations, family discussions and any other time when you want to reduce conflict. Don't say 'but' unless your true intent is to devalue something.

QUICK REFERENCE

What you can do right now:

Make a conscious decision to replace 'but' with 'and' as you talk to yourself and to others. Notice how your thinking 'opens up' as ideas coexist instead of conflict.

Instead of saying,

'I'm getting the hang of my new job, but there are a few things I don't really understand.'

Say,

'I'm getting the hang of my new job, and there are a few things I don't really understand.'

Instead of saying,

'I know you want to expand the sales conference to three full days, **but** consider the budget implications.'

Say,

'I know you want to expand the sales conference to three full days, *and* consider the budget implications.'

Instead of saying,

'I can see that it's a good product, **but** it's expensive.'

Say,

'I can see that it's a good product, *and* it's expensive.'

30. *Let's Do It!*

During a brainstorming/feedback session with your sales team, it becomes clear that there are several points the group is concerned about. One member complains that supervisors in her department ring a bell when incoming calls are waiting, and she finds it distracting. She suggests eliminating the bell.

Say out loud to yourself:

'Well, I'm sorry you don't like hearing it, but it's the only way supervisors can let everyone know that it's time to get back to work. Without the bell, they'd constantly have to walk around gathering up their staff. It's the only practical way to do it.'

Now say:

'I can understand how that would be distracting. Let's find another way to let everyone know when the department is very busy. How about a series of lights up on the wall? If the bell hurts more than it helps, we'll experiment with other techniques.'

Which sounds like a reaction that will encourage more brainstorming ideas, quite possibly leading to innovative breakthroughs? Which will 'block' the participants' creative thinking?

Market researchers often use 'focus groups' to sample customers' feelings about a company's products and services. A dozen or so customers are invited to an informal discussion at a research company and are observed through a one-way mirror. They're told quite openly that company representatives will be watching them, and they're encouraged to say whatever they wish. A chairperson gently guides the discussion, carefully holding back any of his own opinions to avoid influencing the participants' views.

Just after I finished my degree, I was employed by a major advertising agency as an account executive. I handled several multi-million-dollar accounts, including Continental Airlines. Hearing what customers really thought about our ads and the clients' products in focus group sessions was often very revealing. (It was also quite fun watching them from behind that mirror!)

Recently, Stew Leonard, owner of the world's largest dairy store, told me about a focus group session involving several of his store managers and 16 women who had been asked to talk about buying fish.

One woman in the group said,

'I won't buy fish from your shop because I only buy fresh fish, and your's isn't.'

The fish department manager shot to his feet and responded,

'What do you mean it's not fresh? I handle the purchasing myself. We buy fresh fish every single day.'

The woman responded,

'If that's true, then why do you put it in those plastic packets like frozen fish at the supermarket? I like to buy my fish nice and fresh, straight off the ice.'

The shop was already selling 15,000 pounds of fresh fish every week, so it would have been understandable if the fish buyer had set out to convince the woman that she was wrong. Instead, Stew said,

'So she likes her fish on ice. If she thinks it makes such a big difference, let's do it.'

The very next day, they began building a fish display with a bed of ice. The week after installing the 'fish bar', sales doubled! The interesting thing was that sales of the packaged fish did not decline at all. The extra 15,000 pounds of fish sold each week was all new sales, apparently bought by customers who shared that woman's feelings.

It would have been very easy to dismiss the woman's comment about the fish – and miss out on more than three-quarters of a million pounds of fish sales each year.

Positive talkers definitely have strong opinions and aren't afraid to express them – when appropriate. Convincing the other person that your point of view is right can sometimes help you win the battle but lose the war. As a positive talker, you want to make other people feel able to express their ideas and encourage them to think creatively. Only after evaluating the merits of various approaches can you determine the best course of action to take.

One of my clients in the resort development business has been very successful at signing up new members for a national network of private camp-sites. For them, as for most sales organisations, new customers who are referred by existing customers are the most likely to become satisfied customers. The cost of finding them is low, their conversion rate from potential to actual customer is high, and they tend to be happier with their purchases than other non-referred customers. Referred customers have already been influenced by the most powerful form of advertising, word-of-mouth publicity from a satisfied customer.

I watched as my client gathered her employees together and asked them to brainstorm a dozen new ways to increase the flow of referrals. She didn't push her own ideas and she didn't criticise any of their suggestions. In less than 30 minutes, the team had come up with 15 excellent approaches.

This manager was a conscientious user of positive language, an encouraging leader rather than a domineering critic. Her role was to keep saying, 'That's good. I like it. Let's do it. Yes, that could work. Let's think of some more ideas. Keep them coming. Who can see a way to connect these two?'

And when someone else in the group pooh-poohed an idea, she reminded them to keep an open mind.

Encourage other people to cooperate by inviting their input and ideas. Welcome unusual suggestions rather than quashing them. Get all involved parties to contribute their ideas so that creative solutions can result.

QUICK REFERENCE

What you can do right now:

Whenever you seek others' input and suggestions, stimulate a free flow of ideas, no matter how crazy some of them might seem.

Instead of saying,

'I want to give everyone a chance to make one or two suggestions on this project. Please keep our limited budget in mind.'

Say,

'Let's get lots of ideas going. Don't worry about how much they'll cost. We'll consider practicality later. For now, anything goes.'

Instead of saying,

'Your suggestion just won't work. Believe me, I've personally seen it fail at two other companies.'

Say,

'Good suggestion. Let's keep going and come up with some more.'

Instead of saying,

'That's not practical, it'll never work.'

Say,

'That's an unusual approach, let's think about it and see where we end up.'

31. *Do ME a Favour for a Change*

A market researcher for cleaning products phones you at home. After introducing himself, he explains that he's hoping you'll agree to spend about 20 minutes answering his questions.

Say out loud to yourself:

'I was wondering if you could do me a favour and spend 20 minutes answering a few questions about cleaning products. We have this contest going for the market researchers, and I'm really close to winning a trip to EuroDisney for my family.'

Now say:

'We want to continue selling the sort of cleaning products you and your family want. If you agree to take part in our research you'll receive free samples of new products and also have the satisfaction of knowing that you're helping to improve the quality of the products your family use.'

Which approach will motivate you to spend time answering his questions?

There are lots of reasons that motivate people to do business together. Often, they're selfish ones. These can be counterproductive when it comes to encouraging cooperation. Only one reason really counts: the other person must believe that he'll be better off by doing what you suggest.

I'm certainly not against helping a friend. When it comes to a business proposition, though, there's only one party whose interests I'm really looking out for: ME! It's amazing how many salespeople tend to concentrate on why **they'll** be better off if they get you to buy something. As a customer, it's completely irrelevant to me – unless we have a friendship – that you're 'just this close' to meeting your target for the month, or about to qualify for some kind of prize.

When I began presenting sales seminars in the early 1980s, many sales trainers used a popular acronym: WIIFM. The explanation went like this:

'Whenever you're writing a sales presentation, designing an ad or writing copy for a direct mail campaign, only one thing matters: WIIFM! *What's In It For Me?* That's what customers want to know; that's what they're asking themselves as you present your case for what you want them to do. They don't care about a salesperson's company, product features or personal situation. They only care about themselves. They want to know how the action you're suggesting will make them better off.'

A hospital switchboard operator in one of my American seminar audiences recently asked me a question following my presentation.
She said,

'When I ask callers for their insurance information, they often get huffy and indignant. Some of them don't have insurance, and I think they're afraid I won't help them if I find that out. When I tell them I have to get the information for our internal records, they still seem uncooperative. What can I say to make them feel like cooperating?'

I wanted to help her work it out for herself, so I just stood there with my arms crossed and said,

'Why should I want to give you my insurance information?'

She seemed confused, and didn't immediately realise that I was role-playing with her and taking the stance that her callers adopted. I continued,

'I don't care about **your** *internal records or your hospital's requirements. Just tell me why* I *should want to give you the information.'*

She caught on. My point was that she should assume that any caller is constantly asking himself, 'What's In It For Me?'

It took her only a few seconds to come up with the caller-oriented benefit:

'Once I know a little about your insurance cover, I can make sure I'm referring you to the best medical option for your circumstances. If you don't have insurance, I can make arrangements to talk to a public health facility. And if you do, I can determine which of our physicians already have direct billing arrangements with your particular insurance broker, and that can make things much simpler for you by minimising paperwork.'

She got it! Her callers don't care about the hospital at all. They only care about themselves. Before, she was setting out to 'sell' them the value of cooperating with her information request.

Now when she wants to get insurance information from a caller, she can 'sell' them the benefits of cooperating with her question by saying,

'In order to make sure I'm referring you to the physician or facility that's best for your situation, please tell me who your insurance broker is. That way if one of the hospital's doctors has a direct billing arrangement with your company, your paperwork will be minimised later on.'

When you want someone to cooperate, to follow your lead, to do something for you, take off your shoes. Stand in the other person's shoes. Look at the situation from his point of view and show him how he'll benefit by taking the action you recommend.

QUICK REFERENCE

What you can do right now:

When you need someone's cooperation, work out why his participation will benefit *him*, not *you*. Emphasise the benefits he'll gain by following your suggestion.

Instead of saying,

'My son's boy scout group is selling firewood, and if you could just do me a favour and buy two or three sacks, he'll be able to go on the camping trip next month.'

Say,

'My son's boy scout group is selling firewood, and it's really good value. You'll find it burns very well. How much would you like to buy?'

Instead of saying,

'Look, when you interrupt me several times a day with questions, it's almost impossible for me to get any serious work done. Would you do me a favour and save them up so I don't have to keep breaking my concentration?'

Say,

'You deserve my full attention when I'm answering your questions. The best way to get it would be to set up a meeting once or twice a day. That way I'll really be able to concentrate on helping you and cover several questions in depth each time.'

Instead of saying,

'Will you do me a favour?'

Say,

'Here's why this will be good for you.'

32. *You Get What You Ask For*

You arrange a meeting with an important customer because you've heard that he's been talking to one of your competitors. Fearing that you could be about to lose his business, you decide to find out if there's something he's unhappy about.

Say out loud to yourself:

'John, you've been happy with our service, haven't you?'

Now say:

'John, you're a very important customer and my aim is to constantly improve the way we serve you. Which areas would you like us to improve on?'

Which question will encourage your customer to give complete, candid comments? Which will start a conversation that leads to a stronger relationship?

'Hello, Mr Walther, this is Deborah from room service. I'm calling to find out if you were pleased with the pizza we delivered to your room this evening.'

Nobody from any hotel's room service department had ever called me before. Deborah asked me if my pizza had been warm enough, spiced about right, and delivered on time. I said it had been fine. I was surprised at her call and wondered if she had some ulterior motive. Was there some sort of pizza recall? I dismissed the call, got some sleep, and presented my first training seminar for a nearby company the next morning.

The following month I returned to present another seminar for the same company and again stayed at the same hotel. I rarely leave my room the evening before a presentation. Most of the time I order from room service, look through my notes, and get to bed early so I'm fresh for my audience the next morning. I ordered the low calorie chicken dish and enjoyed it. Once again my phone rang after I finished my meal.

'Good evening, Mr Walther, this is Deborah from room service. I'd like to find out if your chicken was prepared to your liking.'

The same young woman had called again. I answered her questions and asked her a few myself. I wanted to know more about why she was calling. Deborah explained that she calls every single guest half an hour after their room service meals are delivered to ensure that things were just right.

I was struck by the simplicity of her approach. Of course! If you want to find out how to improve room service, or any other service, the best thing to do is ask your guest or customer directly. Very few people take the time to fill in those 'guest comment cards' propped up on most hotels' bedside tables. But if you phone guests in their rooms, they'll probably talk to you.

By the time I'd stayed at the hotel seven times, Deborah and I had become quite friendly. I autographed a copy of *Phone Power* and delivered it to her office so I could watch her as she made her calls. Later that evening I listened for two hours in her dingy cubicle beside the service lifts in the sub-basement, where the hotel's kitchen is situated.

Think of all the times you've been served an over-priced, mediocre meal in a restaurant and commented to your companions that the service was poor to boot. Invariably, when the head waiter asks, 'Was everything satisfactory? You enjoyed your meal?' You smile and say, 'Oh yes, thank you, it was fine.' Why didn't you tell him the truth? Perhaps you could sense that he didn't really want to know. His question was a habitual routine – a hollow nicety.

As I sat beside Deborah and listened in on her calls that evening, I noticed that the guests were all quite surprised to hear from her, yet very few offered any really helpful suggestions. Were they really 100 per cent satisfied, or did Deborah's questions themselves need improving?

Most calls went rather like this:

'Hello, Mrs Jones, this is Deborah from room service. I'm calling to find out if you were satisfied with the soup and salad we delivered to your room earlier this evening. Was everything OK?'

The guests nearly always said something like:

'Well, how nice of you to ask! Yes, everything was fine. Thanks for calling.'

After hearing several of these brief conversations, I asked Deborah,

'Do you really just want to know if they were satisfied? Or are you looking for suggestions to help you improve? If you want more helpful comments, let's ask a question that gets to the heart of what you're after. Instead of asking IF THEY ARE HAPPY, let's ask guests HOW WE CAN MAKE THEM HAPPIER. If we've already made them as happy as they can possibly be, they'll say so.'

So, for the next call, Deborah changed her question:

'Good evening, Mr Blackstone. This is Deborah from room service. I hope you enjoyed the steak we delivered to you tonight. I'd like to find out which aspects of your meal could have been a little nicer.'

This took Mr Blackstone by surprise.

'Oh, um, it was very nice. Let's see, how could it have been a little better? Well, the entrée was just right, but I noticed that my bread roll was rather hard. You could check on how fresh they are. It's only a little thing. Everything else was fine.'

Deborah homed in on the bread rolls, and other guests reported that theirs were also a little stale. She contacted the bakery chef, arranged for a new batch, and continued with her calls to help the hotel improve its service.

The best way to reinforce and improve any relationship is to stop and take stock. Whether it's with a customer, a colleague, a spouse, or a friend, find out exactly where you stand and make improvements where needed. When you want to improve any kind of relationship, you must take the time to ask for sincere, candid suggestions about how you can make things better.

Frequently, comments come your way without your even asking for them. They may be critical, and may be couched in harsh terms. When you hear criticism, it's important to let the other party know straight away that you welcome the comments. That doesn't mean that you will necessarily agree with them or find them valid. The important thing is to keep the channels of communication open and show the other person that you respect his viewpoint.

I recommend a two-part conversation. First, say something like,

> **'I'm really glad you're telling me this, and I do want to know how you feel. Thanks for telling me what's worrying you.'**

Then follow up by asking for specifics. Don't dismiss the criticism after hearing the generalities. Instead ask for more.

> **'Please help me understand why you feel this way. What did I do to cause your reaction? I want to be able to watch out for it in the future.'**

Counsellors and therapists constantly remind us to ask how we can improve our relationships. That's good advice. **How you ask** is almost as important as asking. Assume that you could do a better job in some area of your relationship and then ask exactly what that area is. Don't ask if things are OK; ask how you can make them better.

QUICK REFERENCE

What you can do right now:

Make it a habit to ask at least one relationship-improving question every day.

Instead of saying,

> 'Are you feeling reasonably good about our marriage these days?'

Say,

> **'What single thing could I do to be a better marriage partner for you?'**

Instead of saying,

> 'Are you happy with our service?'

Say,

'How could we improve our service for you?'

Instead of saying,

'Have you been pleased with my achievements since you promoted me?'

Say,

'I think I've done pretty well since my promotion, and I want to do even better. Which two or three things could I concentrate on to exceed your expectations?'

Instead of saying,

'Was everything satisfactory?'

Say,

'How can I do a better job for you?'

33. *So, What CAN You Do?*

You work at an airline ticket counter. A tearful woman approaches and explains that she is on her way to visit her grandmother who is very ill, but she has lost her ticket. She asks you for a refund.

Say out loud to yourself:

'No. I can't issue you with a refund. You'll just have to fill in a lost ticket application and wait. You probably won't get an answer for three to four weeks.'

Now say:

'What I can do is issue a replacement ticket and charge it to your credit card. Then I'll help you fill in the lost ticket application and send it on to the appropriate department.'

Which approach is likely to make your agitated passenger feel that you are working cooperatively towards a positive solution? Which will make her feel even more upset?

One morning, while my wife and I were on holiday, we decided to have lunch a little early and went down to the hotel's pool-side restaurant shortly before noon. The place was empty. No one else was seated, and a waiter was arranging cutlery on the tables. The hostess saw us waiting at the entrance and approached with a smile, saying 'We'll be open and ready to begin serving lunch in just a few minutes. I can seat you then.'

The first thought that ran through my mind was, 'If you're going to be open in a few minutes, why don't you just let us sit down at one of those empty tables and wait?' I probably would have argued the point with her had she used the approach I'm more used to hearing: 'The restaurant is closed now and we won't be open for a while. I can't seat you until then.'

What she said carried exactly the same meaning as the more common negative version. Her approach, though, was completely positive, stressing what she **could** do rather than what she couldn't do. Instead of arguing or creating a conflict, Julie and I went to wait in the lounge and enjoy a drink. A few other couples had been greeted with the same smile and positive statement, and they had also gone to the lounge to have drinks. That one hostess had used a positive rephrasing of a negative statement. The end result was that we were all happy to wait, her staff were able to prepare for lunch without interference, and the bar did some extra business!

For every 'can't' statement, there's a 'can'. The negative 'can't' version immediately creates a conflict with the listener. Compare the effect of 'We won't be open this weekend and I'm afraid I can't get your order ready until Monday afternoon' with 'We will be open again on Monday and I'll be glad to have your order ready that afternoon.' The positive version is easier to understand. It also projects a much more friendly, cooperative, helpful impression.

I noticed how a steward described entrée choices on a recent flight. To passengers in the front of the cabin, he offered lasagna, chicken and beef. When he reached my row, the beef was gone. He said,

'Mr Walther, I can offer you the lasagna entrée, which gets lots of compliments, or the chicken dish, which I particularly like myself. Which would you prefer?'

What he didn't say was, 'Oh, I'm afraid we've run out of beef, so I can't offer you that.' By positively describing the alternatives he *did* have available, I felt happy about the choices.

Always choose to use the positive version of a negative statement. Tell people what you *can* do, not what you *can't*. They'll understand you more easily and feel better about what you've told them.

QUICK REFERENCE

What you can do right now:

Whenever you start telling someone what you can't do, substitute a statement describing what you can do.

Instead of saying,

'I can't give you a room with a view of the river tonight; I'll have to put you in one that looks out over the city tonight and move you tomorrow.'

Say,

'I can give you a room with a view of the city tonight and then have you moved into one that looks out over the river tomorrow. That way you'll be able to enjoy both views.'

Instead of saying,

'I can't answer that question for you myself. I'll have to check with customer service and get back to you later.'

Say,

'I can help you with that question by talking to our customer service department. I'll contact you this afternoon to let you know exactly where things stand. What time would you like me to call?'

Instead of saying,

'Here's what I can't do.'

Say,

'Here's what I can do.'

34. *Breaking the Language Barrier*

One of your customers is very upset about a mistake in a recent order. In a highly emotional state, he phones and starts shouting at you.

Say out loud to yourself:

'Well, Chris, it looks as if you have a problem. What do you expect me to do about it?'

Now say this:

'Chris, it's clear that we have a challenge here. Let's see if we can solve it together.'

Which approach is likely to move you towards a solution and create a cooperative atmosphere with Chris?

Part of my work is showing organisations how they can do a better job when dealing with upset customers. One of my assignments involved a car phone company's team of customer service representatives known as the 'Retention Group'. Their job is to 'save' customers who are so unhappy that they've threatened to cancel their car phone accounts. I 'met' Chris B. on my first day of monitoring calls with my new client.

Everyone in the customer service call centre had either been yelled at by Chris B. or had heard stories about his tantrums, demands and verbal abuse. Almost everyone hoped to avoid handling Chris's calls because he was totally unreasonable.

Then along came Mary Hatcher. Her tone of voice, demeanour and superb language skills reassure you that everything's going to be OK. Mary makes things right.

By the time his call was transferred to Mary, Chris B. had already been complaining (vigorously!) for two years about service. She'd heard plenty of stories about him and decided to make him her 'special person'. One of her professional challenges would be to transform this irascible customer.

The first time Chris was transferred to her, Mary got personal:

> 'Chris, I'm familiar with your situation, and I am going to help you. Here's what I've been wondering: how can it be that our service is so terrible, and yet you still remain as one of our customers? Perhaps there's something else that you feel unhappy about. If you're having problems in other areas, the last thing I want to do is add to your discomfort.'

He was taken by surprise. She had immediately cut through the usual business faςade to uncover the root of the problem.

Chris opened up and explained that his business life was a mess. He had problems in his relationships with his employees. He wasn't getting on with his partner. Chris was doing badly on many fronts. His favourite outlet was his car phone, where he could call customer service and unleash a charge-free tirade at someone he'd never have to face.

Chris specialised in erecting barriers. His approach was:

> *'I'm the poor mistreated customer, you're the big rich company making money out of me, and you don't understand what it's like to be on my side of the table. What are you going to do to make up for the way you've mistreated me?'*

Mary specialises in dissolving barriers. Her approach is to get on the customer's side. In fact, she describes her position as being a customer advocate. Her language is filled with obstacle-removing, team-building phrases.

'*We* do have an uncomfortable situation here. *Let's work together and solve this.*'

Instead of permitting a verbal barrier to separate her from the customer, she dissolves it. Rather than trying to convince the customer he's wrong, she validates his feelings and moves on.

'I understand why you feel that way. You have a right to expect good service. Let's find out what's going on so we can solve it.'

Mary's approach works. With her words alone, she showed Chris B. that there was no barrier dividing them. She aligned herself with him, and he calmed down. Other customer service reps started reporting that he was actually sounding nicer when he phoned them. Mary succeeded in changing Chris B. by deciding to dissolve the barrier that he imagined was dividing them.

Most conflict situations involve imagined barriers. When people are working together, on the same side of the table, there's no confrontation. The first challenge in reducing conflicts is to dissolve those barriers. You must show that you want to be a partner, not an adversary.

Be careful to avoid pronouns that contribute to the me/you dichotomy. Use 'we' and 'us' rather than 'you' and 'I' to show that you view your relationship as a partnership.

Be sure to point out any common ground you share. Help the other person see that you truly sympathise with their situation. Once you establish common ground with someone, they're much more likely to treat you as a problem-solving partner rather than an adversary.

Peacemakers like Mary Hatcher are masters at using conflict-reducing language. The principles they use are easy to master, and you'll almost certainly have an opportunity to use them today. Use words that show your counterpart that you want to dissolve barriers and work together.

QUICK REFERENCE

What you can do right now:

When you're involved in a conflict, use your language to show that you're intent on working **with**, not **against** the other person; show that you and your counterpart are on the same side of the table.

Instead of saying,

'It's your problem, what do you expect me to do about it?'

Say,

'We share this challenge, let's solve it together.'

Instead of saying.

'Here's what you'll have to do.'

Say,

'Here's what we can do.'

Instead of saying,

'I understand what you want. But I must stick to my policies.'

Say,

'We share some important goals. Let's see how we can work together to attain them.'

35. *You're Invited!*

Some of your neighbours have decided to fight a local landfill operator's application to triple the size of his site. You want the dump closed. The campaign is going to be expensive. A group of you get together to decide how to proceed.

Say out loud to yourself:

'This is going to cost a lot of money and you'll all have to make donations. You're also going to have to get others in the neighbourhood to contribute, too, unless you can come up with a better idea.'

Now say:

'**We're going to need a lot of money to succeed. We can ask everyone for cash contributions or we can hold some kind of fund-raising event like a big jumble sale and invite the whole neighbourhood to join in. Or we can do something else together. What other approaches can we consider?**'

Which sounds like the tactic that will generate the most cooperation? Which is almost sure to fail?

One challenge I regularly face as a speaker is getting my audience back into the room after each coffee break. Typically, the client or seminar organiser allows 15 minutes for coffee at some point during the presentation. This usually drags on for 25 or 30 minutes, until I remind the organiser that we have a lot of ground to cover and suggest that he reassemble the audience.

Then the organiser goes into the foyer, where everyone is munching biscuits and guzzling coffee. He tries unsuccessfully to get the crowd moving back in, and finally stands on a chair and shouts, 'We're running late. You'll have to return to your seats now.'

I've found a much more effective approach. Just before it's time to begin a break, I say to my audience:

'**Everything is set for our coffee break now, and I'd like you to decide how we'll handle it. We can make it a long break that drags on for 25 or 30 minutes, or we can get straight back to these positive talking techniques and resume the presentation in exactly 15 minutes. Please raise your hand if you prefer . . . .**'

My audiences always choose the shorter break. They didn't come to drink coffee; they want ideas and strategies that they'll be able to put to work – and benefit from –

straight away. I also make a point of saying 'My watch says 12 minutes past 10 now, so we'll start again at 10.27. Enjoy the refreshments, and we'll resume at 10.27.' (My experience has shown that for some reason people pay more attention to odd times. If you schedule a meeting to resume at 10.27, you'll have more people there on time than if you schedule it for 10.30.)

Still, human nature seems to include a herding instinct. Everybody waits for someone else to start moving back into the presenatation room. At my seminars I've found that I'm the best person to play that role. At about 10.25 I move out to the foyer and start the herd moving. Instead of calling out, I approach four or five different clusters of people who are talking to each other and say, 'I invite you to bring your coffee back into the ballroom; we're just about to resume.'

There are two key elements of my audience-assembling technique that make it effective. First, the participants 'own' their course of action. I don't dictate what they'll do, I let them choose. Second, I consciously use the word 'invite'. Nobody likes orders. Everyone likes an invitation. If I were using the more common audience reassembling techniques, people would be thinking,

'Oh, no, do we have to go back in already?'

Instead, these same people look back at me and say,

'Oh, how nice. An invitation. We accept!'

This approach works every time. After all, the audience did come to get as many ideas as possible. I'm using positive talking techniques to help ensure that they get maximum value from the presentation.

Think of the situations you face in your work and daily life. When you want to encourage cooperation, give the other person a role in choosing between the options, and then 'invite' him or her to act on that choice.

Isn't it odd that we so often use the phrase 'have to' when we're inviting somebody to cooperate with us? Those words

141

suggest that the other person has no choice, that the action we're about to describe is mandatory and quite possibly unpleasant.

Friends of ours recently said,

'You'll have to come over for dinner sometime soon.'

We like them, and do want to join them, but it sounded more like a command than a gracious invitation. Soon after, I caught myself saying to other friends,

'We'll have to get together one of these weekends.'

There again, an indication that socialising is more of an unwanted obligation than a preference. It's a lot more inviting to say,

'We'd like to get together with you next week. How about going out to see a film on Friday or lunch at our place on Sunday?'

To encourage cooperation, don't order people to do what you want them to. Invite them to choose between options, so they 'own' their preference.

QUICK REFERENCE

What you can do right now:

When you want others to cooperate with you, 'invite' them to do so and give them a choice about what they'll do.

Instead of saying,

'To be considered, you'll have to take this form, fill it in, and then bring it back in the morning.'

Say,

'You can take this form home tonight and complete it at your convenience. Then, if you like, you can drop it off in the morning.'

Instead of saying,

'You'll have to send the whole unit back to the regional service centre to get it repaired.'

Say,

'You can either send the unit to the regional service centre or take it to a local dealer. Which is more convenient for you?'

Instead of saying,

'Here's what you'll have to do.'

Say,

'I invite you to choose the approach that will work best for you.'

36. *I Recommend*

You sell life insurance and you are talking to a young couple about their needs. Their first child is due in a few months, and the husband plans to buy a substantial life insurance policy. You believe that he should also take out a policy for his wife.

Say out loud to yourself:

'One other thing you might possibly want to consider is buying a policy to cover your wife. Although her health is excellent at present, you never know what might happen during childbirth.'

Now say:

'It's wise of you to provide protection in case you aren't personally able to support your family. Considering the possibility of complications during childbirth, I recommend that you take out temporary cover for your wife as well.'

Which approach is more likely to catch your prospective customer's interest and show that you are genuinely concerned for his welfare? Which is more likely to result in a sale?

That was no hypothetical example; it's exactly what my insurance broker said to me when I recently bought my first insurance policy. I'd always been dead set against buying insurance – until we found out that our first child was on the way.

When I was a child, my dad offered simple advice (to anyone who'd listen) for dealing with life insurance salespeople. He'd say,

> ' . . . and I always tell them I'll buy whatever they suggest, in the amount they think is best, so long as they pay every single premium, including their own commissions.'

Hearing Dad repeat his 'funny' strategy at numerous dinner parties, I learned a clear – and erroneous – lesson about life insurance salespeople: 'Don't ever buy anything from them. They're just after commissions.'

I felt very different when Julie and I found that we were about to become parents. I decided it was finally time for me to arrange insurance protection for her and our baby. I reluctantly took the big step and actually asked for an appointment with a life insurance salesman! I hadn't considered buying a policy for Julie too, but did so after hearing the salesman's recommendation.

After buying the two policies, we decided to have our back garden landscaped to include a nice play area for the baby. The landscaping salesman, after concluding the sale, said,

> **'It's a very small additional investment, and I do recommend that you have us put landscape fabric underneath the ground-cover plants and wood chippings. That will prevent 95 per cent of all weeds and will make sure that you're able to enjoy your garden without having to pull up weeds every weekend.'**

We bought the landscaping fabric.

My life insurance salesman and the landscaper both used a common approach: They 'recommended' a course of action.

'Recommend' is an amazingly powerful word. Whatever your occupation, you sell ideas to others all day long.

Whenever you're selling, make strong use of the word 'recommend'.

I was hired to train a group of telesales professionals who arrange time-share exchanges. One of their goals was to encourage clients to renew their membership early and for longer periods. As I began the training sessions, I noticed that the phone reps commonly used an approach like:

'Oh, incidentally, while I've got you on the line, I notice that your membership will be expiring in another few months, so you might want to start thinking about getting that renewed. And while you're at it, one thing you might possibly want to consider is the cost savings from getting a three- or five-year extension instead of just a single year. Would that perhaps be of interest to you?'

I urged them to stop being so tentative and instead use the CPR sales formula, a sales-closing technique I wrote about in *Phone Power*. Many readers have reported that it works wonderfully and helps them establish positive relationships with their customers.

First, Consult with the customer and ask about his future plans. Does he enjoy using his exchange privileges? Does he have lifetime ownership of his timeshare? Would he like to cut down on paperwork and save money?

Next, the reps Personalise the benefits of a multi-year renewal for that individual caller. They show the member that, considering his personal situation and interests, a multi-year renewal is a better way to go.

Finally, the rep uses the word Recommend to 'close the sale'.

'Mr Barker, for your requirements I recommend the five-year renewal plan. You mentioned that you plan to continue using your exchange privileges, and that you don't want to be bothered with the annual letters and calls reminding you that your membership is about to expire. With the five-year plan, your membership will be renewed, with exchange privileges, for five full years. There's no annual paperwork to bother with and you can't possibly forget to renew each year. I recommend

that we put that through now. Which credit card shall I charge it to for you?'

Soon after the training session, one of the telephone reps called my office and exclaimed,

'It works! It's magic. I've been making sure I say "recommend" in every call, and my sales closing rate is up by 25 per cent.'

'Recommend' isn't magic. And it does work. It works because it's a behavioural trigger. In the case of a salesperson, it's easy to get off track and focus on your own needs rather than the customers'. You may start thinking about your colleagues' sales, your product training, your commission cheques, and everything except what matters most: your customers' needs.

Using the word 'recommend' reminds salespeople that their role is to act as the customers' partner. The timeshare rep's success wasn't due to his use of a magic word. It was a result of focusing on the customer, asking about his needs, and matching them with the benefits of the company's long-term renewal plan.

Make 'Recommend' an important part of your closing argument when selling a product, service or idea. By practising the CPR approach and emphasising the 'recommend' step, you will be putting your concentration where it belongs: on the other person's welfare.

QUICK REFERENCE

What you can do right now:

Whenever you set out to 'sell' an idea, service or product, focus on the benefits to the other person and use the word 'recommend' to close the sale.

Instead of saying,

'Would you be interested in renewing?'

Say,

'Based on what you've told me, I recommend that you renew now and avoid the price increase that's due to be brought in on 15 September.'

Instead of saying,

'I want to sell you . . . .'

Say,

'I recommend that you buy . . . .'

Instead of saying,

'One thing you might possibly want to consider is to
. . . .'

Say,

'I recommend that you . . . .'

37. *What Sounds Fair to You?*

Your neighbour has two large cedar trees on his side of the fence that separates your two houses. One of the trees looks as if it's dying. As it provides privacy for your patio, you want to keep it alive. He's shown little interest in taking action, so you call in a tree surgeon and find that a deep-root fertiliser injection will cost £80. You think your neighbour should pay, as it's his tree.

Say out loud to yourself:

'Look, you don't seem to care much about saving your cedar tree. It's obviously about to die. The tree surgeon says it will cost £80 to fertilise it and I think you should take responsibility for keeping it alive.'

Now say:

'I've noticed that the big cedar tree isn't doing very well. I know you're busy, so when I saw all the brown needles, I contacted a tree surgeon to find out if it could be saved. They say it'll cost about £80. The tree is on your property and we both benefit from the privacy it provides. What

do you think would be the fairest way to handle the expense?'

Which sounds like the approach that will lead to a favourable outcome you're both going to be happy about? Which will make your neighbour think about putting up a tall fence and suggesting that you keep your nose on your own side of it?

Donna, a manager at a well-known office copier company, called my office to inquire about purchasing *Phone Power* audio and video tapes for all her dealers. She wanted to help the independent retailers use effective telemarketing to sell copiers and supplies. This is an excellent strategy for many companies that rely on a network of independent dealers and distributors. When you help your dealers become more profitable, they buy more of your products as they succeed and their business grows.

From our first phone conversation, I felt that Donna would be difficult to deal with. She was intent on getting a special price for everything. I respect people who want to get the best possible value, but in her case there was something rather too pushy about her approach. I explained that she would receive a 30 per cent discount if her order exceeded 250 individual tapes. She wanted 225, which qualified her for a 25 per cent discount. She eventually placed an order for 250 items. I felt confident sending her the tapes together with an invoice, since the company is a very large and reputable one.

Three months later the invoice remained unpaid, though Donna had told me repeatedly that it was 'in the process' of being handled. Then along came a box containing 25 of the tapes. Her handwritten note said,

'I'm returning these 25 tapes for credit. Please reissue the invoice and it will be paid promptly.'

My first reaction was to think to myself:

'What a con. She really only wanted 225 in the first place. She sat on the bill for three months, sent back the 25 that had qualified her for the lower price, and now she expects me to give her a full credit for them so she'll still get the 30 per cent discount on her 225. She's not going to get away with this!'

Here I was, getting all worked up over her attempt to take advantage of me. I thought of writing a 'What kind of fool do you think I am?' letter. Then I thought of confronting her on the phone and telling her she wouldn't get away with her cheap tricks. And then I stopped for a minute and calmed down. The total amount of money at stake was a little less than £100. And I didn't really know that she wanted to take advantage of me, I just assumed it, based on my reading of her personality.

I realised that the £100 wasn't my concern, I just wanted to be treated fairly. She was holding all the cards, though, since she hadn't yet paid a penny. Was the extra money my top priority? No. My real objectives were to: (1) Feel good about the transaction, (2) Keep the door open for a future relationship with the company, and (3) Get paid. All those objectives were dependent on her feeling good about working with me. Rather than writing a nasty letter or having a telephone confrontation, I decided to use a positive approach. In situations like this one, good questions get you a lot further than strong statements.

I phoned Donna the next morning and said:

'Hello, Donna. I got the 25 tapes you sent back. Thanks for packing them so carefully. They were in good condition. I also got your note asking for a corrected invoice. I'd like your advice. Your original invoice included a 30 per cent discount, based on 250 tapes. If you had ordered only 225 in the first place, you would have earned a 25 per cent discount. I don't charge any restocking fee or other penalty for handling your return, and I have been waiting for three months to get your payment. Please tell me what you think would be the fairest way to handle this.'

Presented with these facts, she thought for a moment and said,

'Well, I'd like the 30 per cent discount, of course, but I

suppose the fairest thing would be for you to re-invoice me at the 25 per cent discount.'

If she had insisted that the 30 per cent discount was fair, I would have issued the new invoice without quibbling. As it was, I sent her a bonus gift with her invoice since I felt good about working with her.

The point is this: almost everyone will treat you fairly if you give them a chance. Positive talkers keep the big picture in mind. They don't worry about the minute details. They think of the relationship. What counts in the end is feeling good. If you win the extra £100 and create an unhappy customer who feels she's been treated unfairly, it's not worth it. If you exchange one minute of happiness for a minute of thinking nasty thoughts about someone, you lose. Instead of confronting other people, work with them.

QUICK REFERENCE

What you can do right now:

Whenever you feel that people are about to treat you unjustly, appeal to their own sense of fairness. In the few cases where they continue to act unfairly, forget about it.
Instead of saying,

> 'Your mechanic replaced my brakes three weeks ago and now they've developed a new squeaking sound. Don't try to tell me that it has nothing to do with your work. I expect you to repair it.'

Say,

> **'You did a good job replacing the brakes on my car three weeks ago. Now I've begun noticing a squeaking sound that wasn't there before I brought it in. What would be the fairest thing to do about it?'**

Instead of saying,

'I've lost my receipt, but I bought this lawn mower from your shop less than a month ago. Now it's already broken. I still have the box it came in, with the name of your shop on it, and I demand that you give me a refund.'

Say,

'A month ago I bought this lawn mower from your shop, and unfortunately it's already broken. I do have the original box with the name of your shop on it and I don't have the receipt. What do you think would be the fairest way to handle this?'

Instead of saying,

'I know my rights, and I demand that you do the following . . .'

Say,

'Considering the facts, what would be the fairest way to handle this?'

38. *Let's Look at This Another Way*

As sales manager, you've been asked to select new office furniture for your department. After evaluating several suppliers, you decide that a movable cubicle design is best, and you select one with four-foot-high partition walls. Before you sign the purchase order, the admin manager takes you aside and says, 'It all looks fine except that I disagree with your choice of partitions. Those short ones just don't give enough privacy. We should definitely go for the six-foot-high walls.'

Say out loud to yourself:

'Cynthia, I disagree. The six-foot-high partitions cut people off from each other, and that creates a less cohesive atmosphere in the department. When people feel isolated, productivity is bound to fall.'

Now say:

> **'I understand that you favour higher partitions, Cynthia, and I'd like to consider another point of view. True, the higher partitions create a more private atmosphere, and that can be good in many situations. Other sales managers have reported that their supervisors find it more difficult to keep an eye on their employees when they're cut off from them. In other words, the privacy provided by higher walls can lead to lower productivity. With increased profit targets in mind, we need to consider that factor too.'**

Which approach will lead to more cooperative dialogue? Which will result in each party digging in her heels and defending her own choice?

As co-chair of a major trade association conference's planning committee, one of my jobs was to encourage innovative suggestions from committee members. One of them, Jason, had a reputation for coming up with zany, inspired ideas.

This particular conference has always begun with a Friday-afternoon 'Welcome' speech, followed by a brief cocktail reception, and then 'Dinner on Your Own'. Participants are supposed to have an early dinner, get a good night's sleep, and then wake up alert and ready to go to the first session early on Saturday morning.

In past years the Friday-night activities have caused lots of complaints. Those who arrive early at the cocktail party think of the fancy hors d'oeuvres as their dinner. Late arrivals find long queues and empty hors d'oeuvres trays. So Jason said,

> *'I know! Since the conference is near the beach, we'll have a beach party. We'll serve hamburgers and beer, play Beach Boys music and everyone will get plenty to eat. It will cost a lot less than those fancy canapés, too.'*

The committee agreed that Jason had come up with a wonderful idea, and he immediately started making the arrangements. Two months later, the association's president heard about it. My co-chair and I both received urgent messages on our telephone answering machines:

'I totally disagree with this beach party idea. It's got to be stopped. I don't want everybody staying out late and then stumbling in, all hung-over, for our Saturday morning sessions.'

I felt resistant as soon as I heard the third word of his message. I thought to myself,

'He appoints a committee, gives us a job, and we do it beautifully. Then he comes along two months later and tells us that what we've done is all wrong. He can plan his own conference.'

My co-chair, Janet, acted as peacemaker. I don't think she knows the word 'disagree'. She doesn't use it, and as a result, people listen to her.

'George, I understand what he's concerned about, and this is another point of view we need to consider. He has a good point about the drinking and staying out late. We don't want people to feel sleepy and hung-over when they come in to that first session the next morning. Still, Jason's idea sounds like great fun.'

We realised that the president didn't object to the beach party itself; he was concerned about the late-night row-diness. Our real challenge was to find a way to have fun on Friday night, let Jason know that we appreciated his creativity, and ensure that everybody would be fresh and alert in the morning.

It didn't take Janet long to come up with the solution: have the beach party, issue each person with two drink tickets rather than having an open bar, and close it all down at 10 p.m. That plan would meet every requirement.

When she talked to the president, Janet didn't say,

'The committee disagrees with your idea of cancelling the beach party.'

Instead she began,

'We understand your concern about having a late-night party, and we agree that that's not what we want. Instead of just cancelling the beach party, let's consider some other options.'

It looked as if we were all going to have a good (but not too good) time ... until the local officer of the association said he **disagreed** with the revised plan.

Nobody wants to be condemned or judged unfavourably; they stiffen, resist, and become combative when told that you 'disagree' with them. Though you may not mean it that way, the other person is likely to 'hear' that you are judging him and labelling his way of thinking as wrong.

Validate others' views and let them exist alongside your own. Instead of saying, 'I disagree with you,' you'll find people much more cooperative when you say, 'I understand your point of view, and I have another interpretation I'd like to discuss.'

QUICK REFERENCE

What you can do right now:

Rather than suggesting that someone else's viewpoint is less valid than your own, accept new ideas and let them coexist alongside yours. Then explore the merits of both approaches and come up with an even stronger alternative.

Instead of saying,

'I disagree with your choice of that firm as our official car hire company. They are too expensive.'

Say,

'I understand why you've chosen that firm as our official car hire company. Considering our current budget constraints, let's talk about some other options too.'

Instead of saying,

'I think you're wrong about that colour. A black bathroom would look vile.'

Say,

'I understand that you like the idea of a really unusual colour scheme for the bathroom. Painting it black would be one way of doing it, and there are some other colours that would also look very striking.'

Instead of saying,

'I disagree with you.'

Say,

'I understand, and I'd like to consider some other possibilities.'

VI. *SPEAK DECISIVELY*

WHEN you listen to a positive talker, you hear someone who gets straight to the point, does away with unnecessary verbiage, and says exactly what he means. There's so much waffle around these days that it's a real relief to find someone who gets rid of unnecessary words and concentrates on communicating concisely and precisely.

Positive talkers are definite about what they say. They make commitments about what they **will** do, not what they'll see if they can perhaps possibly try to do. They're always conscious of projecting an image of reliability.

Communication works both ways, and positive talkers listen actively in addition to expressing themselves well. They don't, however, trust that they understand everything perfectly the first time. They demonstrate their communication skills by taking care to verify that what they have understood is, in fact, what you think you said.

In this section you'll met people who manifest their reliability with their language. They show their communication skills by confirming their understanding when they're listening, and by using words efficiently and effectively when they're speaking.

39. *You Should – Or You WILL?*

While on holiday in the Caribbean, you decide to order a box of tropical fruit and have it sent to some friends at home.

The sales assistant says:

'Your gift should get to London in about a week.'

Notice the difference if the assistant says:

'Your gift will arrive in London within five working days.'

Which sounds as if your friends are definitely going to get their fruit before it rots? Which version leaves you feeling rather anxious about when it's going to arrive?

The salesman returning my phone call said,

'As I said when I took the order, your shutters should be ready in two weeks.'

But I had ordered them two and a half weeks ago! The more I deal with people, the more convinced I am that first impressions are very accurate.

The shutter company's leaflets had been distributed throughout our neighbourhood, advertising 'Any size shutter measured and installed.' I called for an estimate well before Seattle's brief and wonderful summer began. The receptionist told me that 'Ned should call you back by the end of the day.' He didn't. The next day I called again. The receptionist said, 'Well, I don't know why he hasn't rung you. He should get back to you straight after lunch.' I knew he should, but didn't have any faith that he would.

After three days I wrote Ned off as yet another unreliable salesman and called a different shutter company for an estimate. After I had arranged my new appointment, Ned finally called! Though I explained that I'd given up on him and phoned a competitor, he said he'd be in my area the next day and told me he'd stop by at lunchtime.

He didn't. But he did come at 4.30 p.m. and quickly measured all the windows. As Ned's prices were about the same as everyone else's, and he had already taken all the measurements, I gave him the order. He said they should be ready in two weeks.

After two and a half weeks without a word, I called and left a message. No response. Another message. No response. My third message was, 'My shutters are late. Return this call today or cancel my order.' Ned did call me back, apparently oblivious of his promised (and missed) delivery dates. His old standard 'should be ready in two weeks' rang hollow since we'd already passed the two-week point. Time marched on. On the one-month anniversary of our order, I left my final message for Ned:

'Tell Ned he can do whatever he wants with our shutters. I'm going to find someone who can keep a promise and place a new order.'

Ned called back, promising to arrive by 1 p.m. the next afternoon. He eventually arived at 4.45 p.m., discovered that some of the shutters didn't quite fit, altered them with the tools in his truck, and asked for his cheque as he was leaving.

I followed Ned out to the drive and said,

'Ned, I'd like you to know what I think of your service. You took twice as long as you said you would. You ignored most of my repeated phone messages. And you didn't honour a single commitment you made to me. I don't feel that you've treated me well as a customer.'

Hardly noticing my obvious frustration, Ned only said,

'Well, I couldn't help it. With this heat wave, what do you expect? Ninety-nine per cent of my customers are happy, and there's always one per cent that won't ever be pleased, no matter what. What do you want? I'm not going to grovel.'

I then realised that I had been wrong. Ned hadn't broken any promises; he had never made any. He'd never said he **would** do anything, just that he **should**.

QUICK REFERENCE

What you can do right now:

Commit yourself to specific dates, times and amounts. 'Should' avoids commitment and sounds wishy-washy.
Instead of saying,

'That should come to about £40 or £50.'

Say,

'That will cost £49.95.'

Instead of saying,

'You should get this in a few days.'

Say,

'I will post this first thing in the morning.'

Instead of saying,

'We should get this done by ....'

Say,

'We will get this done by ....'

40. *Give Your Word and Then Beat It!*

You work part-time in a local quick-print shop. A customer brings in a large copying job and asks when it will be ready.
Say out loud to yourself:

'Well, I'll probably be able to have it for you later today. I'll try for, oh, probably about 4 p.m.'

Now say:

'I will have it ready for you today before 5 p.m.'

If you were the customer, which statement would you consider more reliable? Which version is more convincing?

I was surprised when the room service waiter said 'We'll have your breakfast delivered to you in 20 minutes.' I admit that I felt a little irritable after my delayed flight, late arrival, and lack of sleep the night before.

I woke at 7 a.m. and immediately phoned in my room service order. The 20-minute delivery time I had been given allowed me just enough time to shower, get dressed, watch the 7.30 news headlines as I ate, and be down in the seminar room by 8 o'clock to set up for my 9 a.m. keynote speech.

By 7.35 I was showered and dressed but still hungry. I phoned room service and asked about my breakfast. 'It's on its way.' By 7.45 I felt impatient and angry. They had already taken twice as long as they'd promised. My morning routine had been thrown out and I didn't like it. Each minute that I waited seemed like ten. Finally, at 7.51, the waiter arrived with my tray. The delay probably wasn't his fault, but I told him that he was terribly late and grumbled about how much I resent paying the tips that are automatically added to room service charges.

Was my 46-minute wait for breakfast unreasonable? Not really, except that I'd been promised delivery in 20 minutes. If the person who took my order had said, 'Mr Walther, I'll make sure you have your breakfast before 8 a.m.,' I would have been pleased that it was delivered a few minutes early.

My displeasure was caused by the gap between my expectations and the hotel staff's performance. The larger that gap – when it's in a negative direction – the greater my dissatisfaction. If they had promised 45 minutes and delivered in 46, I would hardly have noticed. If they had promised a '10-minute express service' and delivered in 46, I would have been even more unhappy than I was. If they had promised an hour and delivered in 46 minutes, I'd have been pleased.

One of the surest ways of making people happy is to deliver more than you promise. If you phone a mail-order company and buy a sweater, you'll be delighted if it arrives within 10 days – providing they promised delivery within three weeks. If they said you'd have it in a week, you'll be unhappy when it arrives in 10 days. The customers' level of satisfaction is a result of the expectations created by the serving organisation.

People count on us to deliver at least what we promise. They react favourably when we do better than our promises and unfavourably when we fall short. Most often, we set others' expectations by telling them what we foresee happening. When someone asks you for a commitment, there are three ways you can respond:

1. Don't make a commitment – be vague:

'Well, I'll see what I can do, but I'm not really sure when I'll be able to finish the job. Probably towards the end of the week. We'll just have to wait and see.'

Obviously this isn't going to do much for your image as a reliable professional.

2. Make a hopeful commitment that you may not keep:

'I'll try for Wednesday afternoon.'

If you finish on Thursday, instead, you've just created dissatisfaction.

3. Make a commitment that you will at least keep, and may well beat:

'I will finish the job before the end of the day on Friday.'

Now, when you finish on Thursday, you're a hero!

Jimmy Calano co-founded the world's fastest-growing, most-successful seminar organisation, CareerTrack. I got to know Jimmy early in the company's history when I worked as a consultant to their growing telemarketing department. One reason for CareerTrack's enviable success record is the directors' commitment to delivering more than they promise. When he's planning to send a letter, Jimmy always says, 'I'll send it tomorrow,' even though he intends to send it the same day. That way, if there's an unexpected delay, he'll still be keeping his word. Most of the time, though, he beats it, taking the other person by (pleasant) surprise.

George Patton's formula for success was similar:

'Always do more than is required of you.'

The point to remember is this: whenever you establish expectations for others, be certain that you'll at least live up to them. For best results, exceed them.

QUICK REFERENCE

What you can do right now:

Add a 'safety cushion' whenever you make a commitment. Then delight the other person by doing your best to exceed the expectation you've created.

Instead of saying,

'I should be able to finish that report by, oh, let's say the 15th.'

Say,

'I'll definitely have the report finished before the 17th.'

Instead of saying,

'Your order should be in the post by Wednesday, or maybe Thursday.'

Say,

'Your order will be in the post before the weekend.'

Instead of saying,

'I may be able to get round to it by 2 or 3 p.m.'

Say,

'I will get to it before 5 p.m.'

41. *I Think I Understand What You Think You Said*

You've just taken an order from one of your customers, and it's more complicated than usual. He has requested a special delivery address, and the instructions are complex.
Say out loud to yourself:

'OK, I'm pretty sure I've got that right.'

Now say:

'Can I just go through those directions again to be sure I've understood you correctly?'

Which version demonstrates to your customer that you really care about getting things right? Which order is more likely to go astray, get delayed, and ultimately lead to an unhappy buyer?

An American company called General Foods markets different types of coffee in little 4.5-ounce tins that cost rather a lot. 'Suisse Mocha' and 'Café Franɔais' are my favourites, and Julie and I get through a great many tins every month. I wish the company would sell the same stuff in larger tins at a lower cost per serving. It annoys me that a substantial portion of the price goes to pay for the container itself. If they sold the product in five-pound tins at my local supermarket, I'd happily buy it.

Many of the foods we purchase today, and many other products, for that matter, have a freephone number printed somewhere on the packaging. Companies like General Foods rely heavily on customer input in order to improve their products, clear up confusion, and respond to rumours and crises. If you open a tin of food and find bits of metal inside, the manufacturer wants to know about it immediately. Prominently displaying their freephone numbers is a defensive strategy for organisations that want to hear about – and solve – potentially costly problems before they escalate.

As I waited for the microwave to boil my last cup from yet another Suisse Mocha can, I called the General Foods freephone number to ask if the company had considered selling its coffee in larger containers. A very polite young man called Jerry at the customer service response centre answered and sounded genuinely interested in my views. He stressed that input like mine was exactly what helps the company decide how to change and improve its products.

After explaining why only small cans are used (freshness!), and checking to see if there was anything else I wanted to comment on, he explained that his marketing department keeps track of which parts of the country call with what types of questions. He asked for my address and telephone number. After I told him, he said,

'Can I just check that I've taken this down correctly?'

and proceeded to repeat exactly what I had just told him.

The simple fact that he verified my address showed me that he takes pride in doing his work professionally. General Foods must genuinely care about getting things right if they've taken the time to train their reps so carefully.

It's easy to think,

'Well, so what? So he verified an address. Why is that even worth mentioning in this book?'

The image you personally project to others and to yourself is composed of many small elements. General Foods' image is built from advertising slogans, the colours its designers choose for the coffee can labels, the way the customer response centre staff answer your calls, and yes, even the way Jerry verified my address. Each element contributes to the overall impression.

The technique Jerry used to confirm my address also delivered a message to himself. He said he was checking ' . . . to make sure that I've taken this down correctly.' The message he sent to himself was:

'I'm a professional. I get things right because I take the time and trouble to double-check even something simple like an address.'

I also noticed that his phrasing avoided any possibilty of my 'hearing' him questioning my communication abilities. Had I spoken inarticulately and garbled my words, Jerry might well have said,

'Um, it's so hard to understand you. I'd better check to make sure you were saying what you meant to say.'

He could have asked for verification in a way that I might have interpreted as an accusation that I wasn't speaking clearly. Jerry, however, took full personal responsibility for getting the address right.

Professionals like Jerry inspire confidence and respect with everything they do, right down to the way they verify an address. Take the extra step of checking your communications with others to ensure that you also project a thorough, professional image. And do it in a way that shows you acknowledge your own responsibility for communicating clearly.

QUICK REFERENCE

What you can do right now:

Take an extra moment to check that you have understood accurately. Do it in a way that shows you accept responsibility for getting the information right.

Instead of saying,

'Your accent is hard to understand – I'm not sure I've got that right.'

Say,

'I want to check that I've understood you clearly.'

Instead of saying,

'I think I've got that straight. If I get lost on the way, I'll phone you.'

Say,

'Can I just check that I have those directions all straight? That way I'll be sure to arrive on time.'

Instead of saying,

'I suppose that covers it. I think we understand each other.'

Say,

'Let's check that we're both in complete agreement by running through the points we've discussed.'

42. *Don't Take 'No' – or 'Yes' – for an Answer*

Your neighbours have invited you out for a picnic. The day before, you call to see what you can contribute.

Say out loud to yourself:

'Is there anything I can bring?'

Now say,

'What's the best thing for me to bring?'

What sounds like you really want to bring something? Which question is most likely to trigger the usual – though not necessarily truthful – response, 'Nothing at all, just bring yourselves'?

One of the most challenging tasks any sales trainer faces is getting salespeople to stop asking Yes/No questions. Using multiple-choice and open-ended queries helps reveal the real reasons for buying.

One of my clients sells 'voice mail' for car phone customers. Portable phones are great, providing you're always available to answer calls. Most people who buy and use them do so because 'being in touch' is vital in their business. While they are driving, car phone users are often talking on the phone, thus blocking incoming calls, unless they have a 'call waiting' feature. In other words, people often don't get the constant availability they really want when they invest in a car phone.

That's where the voice mail service comes in. With this service, callers are always greeted by the car phone subscriber's voice. If he's already using the phone or has his phone turned off, the caller hears a recorded message saying:

'Sorry, I'm either using my phone or am not available at present. Please leave a message after the tone and I'll get back to you shortly.'

This service costs very little and tremendously increases the value of having a car phone. Still, the customer service reps working for my client weren't doing very well at selling the voice mail service.

What were they doing? Asking Yes/No questions.

'Are you interested in getting a voice mail service to go with your car phone?'

Of course most people said no without even understanding what the service was. Once they've heard a prospective customer say no, most salespeople get discouraged and move on to the next call.

I was asked to train my client's telemarketing staff to do a better job of selling this valuable service. We began by focusing on questions. After a short brainstorming session, we had over 20 open-ended and multiple-choice questions scrawled on the flip chart, such as 'How do you use your car phone in your business?' and 'When people say they have trouble reaching you on your car phone, is it usually because you're away from the phone and don't answer, or because you're already using the phone, so they get an engaged signal?'

After shifting away from Yes/No questions to the open-ended and multiple-choice varieties, sales statistics more than doubled. Many of the reps reported that once they asked the right questions, their customers quickly sold themselves on the benefits of using the voice mail service.

You ask questions to get information. Yes/No questions give you very little. When you want good information, ask good questions.

When your best friend comes home from hospital after minor surgery, you really want to know how you can help. If you ask a Yes/No question,

'Is there anything I can do?'

the answer will probably be no. To be a more helpful friend, use a different type of question:

'What's the one thing you'd most like me to do to help you?'

Get into the habit of replacing Yes/No questions with multiple-choice and open-ended queries. They produce much more useful information for you to act on.

QUICK REFERENCE

What you can do right now?

Whenever you ask someone a question, first ask yourself, 'Is this a Yes/No question?' If it is, change it to the multiple-choice or open-ended variety.

Instead of saying,

'Is there anything I can get for you when I go to the shops?'

Say,

'What can I pick up for you when I go to the shops?'

Instead of saying,

'I'm considering giving Mark a job at my company. Does he have any particular strengths or weaknesses I should know about?'

Say,

'As I consider Mark for a job at my company, which of his personal strengths and weaknesses should I bear in mind?'

Instead of saying,

'Are there any features you really want in a new computer?'

Say,

'What are the features you really want in a new computer?'

Instead of saying,

'Do you have any questions?'

Say,

'What questions do you have?'

43. *Say It!*

You're being interviewed for a new job and the personnel director asks about your achievements in your previous job. Say out loud to yourself:

'Well, I'm glad you asked that question. First of all, one thing I'd like to say is that, generally speaking, my department was a bit of a mess before I took over. Within six months, more or less, it ran fairly smoothly.'

Now say:

'My proudest achievement was reorganising my department. It was very disorganised when I was promoted to manager. Over the first six months we implemented an action plan that cut unnecessary paperwork by 30 per cent.'

Which sounds like the person you'd consider more seriously for the position? Who seems to be beating around the bush?

I sat in on an American client's meeting with his lawyer and was amazed at how little was said, and how many words it took to say it. The client wanted to know if it was legally permissible to tape-record phone conversations between employees and customers. This is a complicated issue, as state and federal regulations may both come into play. Still, the answer should have come pretty close to 'Yes' or 'No'.

Instead, the lawyer rambled on:

'Well, that's a very interesting issue you've raised, and I'd like to give you my views on it. You must understand, of course, that this is just my opinion at this point in time. I would tend to think that – and keep in mind, of course, that this question is subject to a number of interpretations – it would be quite common to assume that certain legal considerations do have some bearing on an employer's ability to do so. Now, let me ask you something. What I would like to know is . . . .'

I stopped listening and so did the client. Why couldn't the lawyer just say, 'Yes, if you have a beep tone on the line.' Or, 'No, not under any circumstances.' Or even, 'Yes and no: for calls to customers in another state, the more liberal federal regulations do permit taping; for calls within a state, you may not record conversations under any circumstances.'

I suppose, if you're paid by the hour – and thus by the word – it makes sense to beat around the bush for a while. All those lawyer jokes must have sprung from clients' first-hand experiences. They're not all loquacious, of course. My own lawyer gets high marks for giving clear, concise answers. (Thank you, Scott!)

I'm not trying to pick on lawyers; a lot of people talk a lot without saying much. I'll list some of my favourite gripes here, and you'll probably think of a dozen other examples to add.

At this point in time. Doesn't that mean 'now'? I have a business associate who invariably uses this phrase. The only justification I can come up with is that he may think it sounds a little more formal than 'now'. But it doesn't. It makes him sound self-important. For the phrase 'at that point in time', substitute 'then'. Whenever you can say something in fewer, simpler words, do.

Can I ask you a question? You just have! Why make one question into two? When the time is right, ask. You don't need to ask permission to ask a question.

Can I interrupt you? The best strategy is always to hear the other person out and then respond. If someone is wandering off the point, it's better to interject your comment politely without first asking permission.

I would tend to think that . . . Sounds wishy-washy. Say what you believe without first setting up a safety cushion to cover yourself in case your opinion proves unpopular or wrong.

I was going to say . . . This phrase adds nothing and may well undermine the impact of what the person goes on to say. It's rather like saying 'It was just a thought, and it may not be worth bringing up, but I suppose I will anyway, so here's what I was going to say.'

Kind of, sort of . . . There are a great many of these vague qualifying phrases that diminish the impact of what people have to say. These indefinite qualifiers add nothing to your meaning: get rid of them!

May I ask who's calling? Flying to a speaking engagement in Canada, I sat beside Gene Monroe, Vice-Chairman of a large business equipment supplier. He saw me working on the manuscript for this book and asked what it was about. As soon as I told him, he said,

> *'What I really hate is having someone ask if it's OK to ask who I am. I always say no. That really throws them. Why do they ask the question if they aren't prepared to deal with the answer?'*

Secretaries seem to give little thought to their questions about a caller's identity. If you're greeted with, 'May I tell him who's calling?' and the secretary later returns to the line and tells you that he's in a meeting, don't you immediately suspect that you've been deemed Not Important Enough to be put through? A much more effective and courteous way to ask is to explain the benefit to the caller: 'Please give me your name so I can prepare him for your call or arrange for him to call you back.'

I would say ... Are you going to? Why not just say it? Is there an 'if' upon which the statement depends? What does the conditional 'would' contribute anyway?

Can you spell your name? One of my favourites! I'm always tempted to answer, 'Yes. In fact I learned how several years ago, and I've become quite good at it.' What you really want to know is how the name is spelt, so I recommend making your real request politely: 'Please spell your name for me.'

There's a great need for straight talking in business. Think of the phone bills, paper, postage and computer time that we could save if people just said what they meant. And the meetings! I'm an advocate of stand-up meetings. I've heard waste-conscious managers say that all chairs should be removed before routine staff meetings. It's just too easy to settle down for a long session half-listening to people verbally wander. You can sit in a chair fairly comfortably for 60 to 90 minutes; you can stand on your feet for about half as long. People get to the point faster when they're on their feet.

Speaking economically and decisively doesn't just save time; it also inspires confidence in your listener. When you use lots of unnecessary words, it can seem as if you're trying to hide something, or as if you're really not sure of what you're saying.

Sales reps at a telephone company I know of are trained to reinforce customers' purchase decisions with decisive, benefit-oriented statements. Rather than saying,

'I think this will probably work out pretty well for you. Hopefully, this service should give you just what you're after.'

trainers stress the importance of making unequivocal statements:

'This is going to be just right for you. I know you'll find that this service is exactly what you need.'

The word, 'hopefully', in itself, undermines any chance of sounding decisive.

'Hopefully this will change things.'

doesn't offer much hope. It's much better to say,

'This will improve your situation.'

A positive talker is not cold, unfriendly, mean with words, or mechanical in his style of communication. He's someone who does away with unnecessary verbiage, makes his point, and moves on. There's a big difference between patiently comforting a friend who is in trouble and raising a question or making a point in business. A positive talker is flexible and uses the style of communication that's appropriate to the situation.

QUICK REFERENCE

What you can do right now:

Know what you want to say and say it!
Instead of saying,

'One thing I'd like to say is . . . .'

Say it!

Instead of saying,

'Do you mind if I ask you a question?'

Ask it!

Instead of saying,

'Well, generally speaking, one thing I would tend to think is . . . .'

Say,

'I believe . . . .'

VII. *TELL THE TRUTH*

POSITIVE talkers prize integrity. People who are dishonest may feel that they get more rewards out of life than those who are always truthful. They may cheat to buy happiness. Though tangible wealth may contribute to happiness, material possessions are not the yardstick of true success. Many of the world's financially super-rich people are emotionally destitute. In the end, the good guys do win. Do you know any dishonest people who are truly happy?

Positive talkers let you know that they are 100 per cent honest by eliminating integrity-destroying phrases such as 'To tell you the truth.' When someone says, 'Well, to be absolutely honest with you . . .,' don't you think to yourself, 'Does that mean that he's usually not honest?'

In the following chapters, you'll be reminded of the great benefits of being consistently honest. You'll also see how difficult it is to conceal basic dishonesty. As a positive talker, you constantly affirm your integrity with your choice of expressions and mode of speech.

44. *To Be Honest with You*

You've just met an investment consultant who wants to win your trust and your business. You ask him about the performance of his own investment portfolio, and he responds,

'Well, to be perfectly honest . . . .'

Which way do you run?

In my first conversation with Mr M., a promoter who booked me for a series of public seminars, he said,

'We're going to try and book the new opera house for your presentation. To tell you the truth, we could sell all 1000 seats for each of the three seminars.'

I'm immediately wary when someone prefaces supposedly truthful statements with phrases like, 'To tell you the truth . . . .' If a person is habitually honest, if his integrity is 100 per cent, why should he make a point of explaining that he's about to tell the truth?

A month before the presentation, he phoned me to explain that ticket sales were disastrous:

'Well, to be completely honest with you, our marketing information was slightly inaccurate and we may have to start from scratch. Could we possibly push the date back a couple of weeks?'

One peculiarity I noticed about this promoter was that he had no home phone number. In case of a last-minute delay en route to the engagement, I wanted to be able to contact him. Mr M. said his home was his refuge; the phone rang enough during office hours. Later I found out that he didn't have a house. He lived on one floor of his parents' house and used their phone! So much for this big-time promoter.

Each time I asked for an estimate of the audience size, his answer was evasive:

'Well, *frankly, anything could happen. There may be a last-minute surge of sales. Don't worry, we'll invite pupils from the local school to fill any spare seats.*'

Finally, the big day arrived! Julie and I travelled there and were picked up at our hotel in a somewhat shabby rented car. Mr M. apologised,

'*I'm sorry we had to pick you up with the car. Unfortunately, to tell you the truth, the corporate helicopter is taking one of our clients on a sightseeing trip today.*'

(Later it became clear that he and his company didn't even own a beaten-up old Ford, let alone a helicopter.)

'Well,' I said, '*the seminars begin first thing tomorrow morning. How many tickets did you end up selling?*
'*Well, ah, to be completely candid, ah, I don't know the final figure, but ah, to tell you the truth, it looks as if there may be only a couple of hundred.*'
'*For each of the three seminars?*'
'*No, for all three seminars combined.*'
'*Don't tell me you've booked me into a 1000-seat opera house and we'll have less than a hundred people in each audience! It's going to look and feel like a complete flop.*'
'*Oh no, don't worry, we've moved it to a conference room in a nearby hotel that'll be just the right size.*'

The next morning I walked into the conference room, ready to set up my props and adjust the projector. There were only 25 seats. That turned out be OK. Mr M. had sold only 18 tickets!
Part of my agreement with the promoter was that the balance of my speaking fee would be paid before the presentation began. Standing outside the seminar room, he began patting his pockets when I asked for my cheque.

'*Oh um, to tell you the truth, I think I may have forgotten my chequebook.*'

My conversations with Mr M. became interesting performances in themselves. I started to enjoy asking him for a simple, honest answer and then listening to him squirm and wriggle with some phrase that revealed his innate dishonesty.

I did begin presenting the first of my three seminars without the promised payment, and explained that I would not begin the second one until he had visited the bank and secured a banker's draft.

I was surprised when, as I ended the first seminar three hours later, he returned with the strangest-looking cheque I've ever seen. Although it bore none of the usual pre-printed account information, it did have three different signatures scrawled on it, as well as a neatly affixed 'certification label' in the upper left corner. It looked like a case of overkill, as if Mr M. had said to some bank clerk friend:

'Look, to be perfectly honest, this speaker wants a certified cheque, but, well, to tell you the truth, I just won't have the funds until the end of the day. Could you maybe take one of those blank counter cheques and stamp it a few times, and scribble some signatures on it, and stick some kind of label on it so it looks really official?'

The next morning, after completing the three seminars with a grand total of fewer than 100 in the combined audiences (just slightly shy of Mr M.'s 'honest' assurance of 3000), I went to three different branches of the bank on which the suspicious cheque had been drawn. Officers at each one looked at it sceptically and said they'd never seen a cheque quite like it. None would cash it.

It's sad, and true. Completely honest people are rare. Think of all the people you've known. There are a few who always do exactly what they promise, always tell the truth, and are completely trustworthy. And there are many whose honesty is well below 100 per cent.

Even people who have a high sense of personal morality use integrity-destroying phrases. It's a habit that's easy to change – and well worth changing.

Be committed to complete honesty in your behaviour and show it with your language. The rewards for establishing a reputation for 100 per cent integrity last throughout your life. Not only will others be much more willing to work with and trust you, you'll also enjoy the feeling of self-respect that results from knowing you are a person of unwavering character.

QUICK REFERENCE

What you can do right now:

When everything you say is totally honest, there's no need to warn anyone that you're about to tell the truth. Eliminate 'integrity-destroying' expressions that suggest you aren't always sincere and forthright.

Instead of saying,

'To be perfectly honest . . . .'

BE perfectly honest.

Instead of saying,

'Well, to tell you the truth . . . .'

ALWAYS tell the truth.

45. *Just Say No!*

A colleague at work asks you to help him with one of his projects. You're feeling under pressure with your own workload and have no time to spare. Still, you don't want to disappoint him.

Say out loud to yourself:

'I'm awfully busy with my own work, John, but, well, I suppose I could try to help you. I don't know if I'll get round to it, but I'll see what I can do.'

Now say:

'John, I'm completely committed to my own projects at the moment, so I can't help you with yours. I suggest that you ask Tony. He's familiar with your department.'

Which version are you likely to regret later on? Which is the more truthful approach?

My professional speaker colleagues don't usually like clients to videotape their presentations. When they do allow it, they normally charge a substantial fee. Speakers want to avoid the all-too-common situation of a client taping their presentations with poor-quality home video equipment, catching them on an off day, and then distributing the unedited tapes. Thousands may see them and conclude that a speaker isn't very good, based on that one bad tape.

In May 1990 I left my wife and our newborn daughter behind and flew to Detroit to do a free presentation. A member of my staff (since sacked!) had agreed to waive my fee for a seminar promoter, even though his was not a non-profit organisation – the only situation in which I'll give a free speech.

But I believe in keeping my word, and even though the client wasn't a non-profit organisation, he had been promised a free speech by my assistant, and I honoured my employee's commitment. I didn't relish this engagement from the outset, and I had made a commitment.

The week before the presentation, the promoter phoned and offhandedly mentioned that he videotapes all presentations for promotional use. Rather than asking for my permission, he used a ploy commonly used by slick, manipulative salesmen. 'You don't mind, do you?' Instead of telling him how I really felt, I said it would be OK. He agreed that I would be given the only master cassette of the tape and that brief clips from his copy would be used only for promotional purposes.

Immediately after hanging up, my inner voice said,

'Wait a minute, why are you agreeing to this? You didn't want to do this free speech in the first place; there's something fishy about the whole thing.'

Upon my arrival at the hotel, I found just what I had begun to suspect: a very low-budget operation. The promoter was arranging chairs, setting up tables, and attending to administrative details himself. At this point, though, I couldn't turn back. Once I'm there, my responsibility is to the audience. I knew that 650 people were looking forward to that evening's event.

An hour before starting time, a young man named Charlie walked in with his VHS camcorder. He was an old friend of the promoter and had offered to tape all the seminars in exchange for free tickets.

As it was, the presentation went very well. The audience was attentive and responsive, the 'video crew' unobtrusive, and I felt good about my performance. At the end I received an enthusiastic ovation, autographed many books, and saw hundreds of happy audience members head for home, eager to put the seminar ideas into practice.

As the hotel staff began folding up the chairs and tables, I asked Charlie for my video master. He looked surprised and said it belonged to him, but offered to make me a copy. I firmly told him that the master copy was mine, and explained my agreement with the promoter. He said, 'No, I keep the master. It's mine, but you can have a copy if you'd like.'

Charlie was not a timid young man, and insisted quite firmly that the original master tape was his. I insisted that it wasn't.

Then Charlie came up with his hypocrisy jab:

I've just been listening to your seminar, getting great ideas, and admiring you as a superb communicator. At this point, though, I feel that the way you're communicating with me totally contradicts what you've been saying during your speech.'

And Charlie was absolutely right. After several minutes of our tense exchange, he 'got me' with the truth. My behaviour had been inconsistent with what I'd been saying on the stage. As a result, we were having a very uncomfortable exchange. Although we hadn't actually shouted at each other, I had asked him to hand me the master so that

I could stamp on it, thus ending the discussion about who 'owned' it.

Our exchange turned the corner only after I responded to his hypocrisy charge:

'Charlie, you're right. I haven't communicated well with you. I haven't really been honest. The truth is, I feel taken advantage of. I didn't want you to tape me in the first place. I was told only a few days ago that you would be here, and I should have insisted on sticking to my normal agreement that permits taping only with professional equipment, for payment of an additional fee. I haven't felt right about any aspect of your taping and should have denied permission from the start.'

Charlie's face relaxed and he smiled. 'Now I understand,' he said. 'You should have told me that right from the start.'

We finally agreed that he'd send me the original master after making a copy for promotional use only. We spoke to the seminar promoter and reviewed our agreement. And we ended up with a friendly understanding.

The lesson was an obvious one. When you don't want to say yes, don't. I had, and the result was a tense atmosphere and temporary ill-will. Had I stuck to my convictions from the start, I could have avoided the entire confrontation.

When you half-heartedly agree to do something that you really don't want to do, you almost always regret it later. If you aren't sure you really want to do it, it's best to just say no.

While preparing the manuscript for this book, one of my neighbours phoned and asked me to help her with a 'little project'. She wanted help writing a letter to a local property developer. I'm concerned about the development issues she raised, and have already made many contributions to our neighbourhood group. I was tempted to just go ahead and write the letter for her. By the time I'd discussed it with her, revised the draft version, and so on, the 'little project' would have taken at least two hours from my much more important work of writing this book. So I said:

'Sandy, all my time and energy is going into writing my new book at present. I know you'll do a good job of writing the letter on your own. No, I won't help you write it.'

I felt so good about saying no! I wasn't trying to be rude or uncooperative; I was simply drawing the line.

We all take on tasks that we don't really want to do. The result is usually that we do them half-heartedly, feel bad about it, and regret having said yes in the first place. It's much better to say no when that's what you really feel.

QUICK REFERENCE

What you can do right now:

Before you agree to do anything you're only half-sure you want to do, take a few minutes to think about it. Decide if you'll be able to do a good job, enjoy doing it, and finish it without interrupting your other more important priorities. If you decide that you don't really want to do it, say no.

Instead of saying,

'Well, I really don't have time, but I'll see if I can squeeze in an hour or two for you.'

Say,

'No, I'm sorry. You'd be better off getting help from someone who can really get involved.'

Instead of saying,

'Gosh, it's an honour, and I don't know quite what to say. I'm not sure, but I suppose I'll be able to serve on the committee.'

Say,

'Thank you for asking me. I'll carefully assess my workload and other commitments and give you an answer by the end of the day.'

Instead of saying,

'I don't really want to, but I suppose I'll say yes.'

Say,

'No, I won't, though I do appreciate your asking.'

46. *Never Say Always*

You've just bought some more plants for your living room after seeing yet another African violet wither away, just as the fern did two weeks ago, and the philodendron before that.

Say out loud to yourself:

'Everything I try to grow always dies. I can never keep a plant alive for more than a month.'

Now say:

'Some of the plants I've been growing stay fairly healthy for a while, and then I'm not sure what happens. I'm going to buy a book about houseplants and work out what I should be doing differently.'

Which version sounds as if you should just give up and buy artificial flowers? Which shows that you're going to improve on your horticultural track record?

I could see her paper plate tipping 10 degrees, then 15 degrees, then 20 degrees. The wedding was at a yacht club, which didn't explain her listing dish; we were ashore in the club's dining hall. The sixtyish woman in front of me in the queue at the buffet was attractive and vivacious. Her plate was heaped with prawns, roast beef, pasta salad, and, for some reason, a little pile of salted peanuts. She was waiting for – and concentrating on – the champagne being poured as her plate angled precariously. At 25 degrees, the first peanuts started to roll towards me, and I could visualise the whole lot slopping off the plate and on to my shoes.

'Excuse me, your food's just about to spill.'
'Oh, don't mind me. I'm always spilling everything. I'm so clumsy I'm probably going to spill the champagne too! I always do.'

Her self-denigration, though expressed jokingly, left me thinking that her self-esteem must be very low. She probably always says she messes everything up – whether she's talking about cooking, organising her finances, or anything else. Even though she seemed jolly, I felt sorry for this woman. She didn't think much of herself.

You know how uncomfortable it is to be with a couple who are having marital problems. They have a couple of drinks, then start pouring out their mutual disgust.

'If she hadn't made us so late, I'd have helped you with the drinks. She just never can get ready on time. She's always late.'

'Me? He's the one who lost the car keys. He's always losing them. In fact he always loses everything. The first time we went out together he even lost the concert tickets.'

You want to stop them, but it's too late. They've already plunged into inaccurate universals: always, never, everything, nothing.

Universal statements are rarely true and they're hardly ever constructive. Is it possible that he **always** loses the keys, and **everything** else? Does the woman in the queue at the wedding reception **always** spill **everything?**

The most important universal terms to eliminate are the ones you use to describe yourself.

'I can't believe I've done it again! Every time I print out a draft copy of something on the computer, I always forget to switch from the dot matrix printer back to the laser printer. I never get it right. What's the matter with me?'

This kind of self-abuse won't help change the situation. It's much more constructive to replace the universals with more accurate modifiers:

'Sometimes I forget to change the printer switch. I'm getting better at remembering, and I don't always get it right. Now I'm going to concentrate on setting the printer switch correctly.'

Whether commenting on your own behaviour or someone else's, eliminate untrue universal terms and replace them with accurate descriptions of what's really happening. You'll be doing yourself justice and encouraging others to cooperate with you too.

QUICK REFERENCE

What you can do right now:

Look out for and eliminate universal terms like 'always', 'never', 'everything' and 'nothing', especially when using them to criticise someone else's performance or your own.
Instead of saying,

'I can never remember your phone number.'

Say,

'Sometimes I have trouble remembering your number, so I'm going to write it down in my address book.'

Instead of saying,

'You always go too close to the back wall when you put the car in the garage. Can't you ever get it right?'

Say,

'When you leave plenty of room in front of the car, it's much easier for me to get at my workbench.'

Instead of saying to yourself,

'Everything goes wrong every time I try to negotiate with him. I always end up giving in and I never get treated fairly.'

Say,

'Sometimes my negotiating techniques haven't resulted in a positive outcome. Next time I'm going to use another approach.'

VIII. *GET BACK TO BASICS*

WINSTON Churchill was right when he said, 'All the great things are simple. . . .'

Having got this far in *Say What You Mean and Get What You Want*, you've probably said to yourself many times, 'These techniques are so simple!' And indeed they are. Positive talkers aren't particularly skilled at making things complicated; they don't employ any mysterious tricks. They are careful to speak positively, express appreciation, be optimistic, accept responsibility, be cooperative, say exactly what they mean, and tell the truth.

That's about all there is to it, except for three more basics: *Get people's names right, say 'Please' and 'Thank You', and when you're wrong, say you're sorry.*

This last section doesn't need any introduction. If you were uneven in your application of the preceding 46 techniques, and just made sure you always remembered these last three, you'd be a long way ahead of most people. Positive talkers remember the basics.

47. *The Name Game*

Waiting to be seated at a restaurant, you vaguely recognise another diner who gets up and approaches you. His name doesn't come to mind.

Say out loud to yourself:

'I'm terribly sorry. I know I should remember your name, but I just can't think of it.'

Now say:

'It's nice to see you, I'm . . . .'

Which is the more socially confident version? Which statement sounds more self-assured and which sounds weak?

I was shopping at an office supplies shop, sampling the various felt pens, when a familiar-looking woman came up and said, 'Hello! I thought I recognised you.'

I used to feel awkward when I didn't remember someone's name. I'd launch into the old 'don't-hurt-their-feelings' excuses you hear all the time. Realistically, though, even a memory expert doesn't remember everybody's name. You and I definitely don't. When you've forgotten someone's name, do away with unnecessary verbiage, avoid belittling yourself, and always tell the truth.

I realised that I wouldn't remember this woman's name. As I opened my mouth, prepared to say,

'Please remind me of your name,'

she cut me off, saying,

'George, I'm Sandy Wilson, from PNSA. It's nice to see you.'

Of course! I know Sandy and have talked to her on the phone and at meetings several times. She didn't leave me in the awkward position of having to explain that I'd forgotten who she was.

We skipped over the usual chitchat about forgetting names and renewed our acquaintance quickly. I admired Sandy for taking the initiative.

When you deal with people, names are important. Fortunately, when you attend a conference, delegates usually wear badges proclaiming their names. You can discreetly glance down (as they do, too) and refresh your memory, maybe even appearing to have remembered on your own. But in real life you often have to ask.

One key to building a rapport with other people lies in knowing and using their names. Everyone loves the sound of their own name, and developing a talent for remembering and using names can be a tremendous asset in business. You can easily excel in each of the three most common situations that come up when dealing with names: when you've forgotten theirs, when they've forgotten yours, and when you've first met (and not yet forgotten).

1. Don't Lose Face Over a Forgotten Name.
The best way to handle forgetting a name is very simple. Accept it! You've forgotten a name – so what? Why worry about it? The other person may have forgotten yours too, and has certainly forgotten plenty of others'.

The next time you go to a party, bump into a long-forgotten colleague or customer at the airport, or end up in the Safeway queue behind a new neighbour you've recently met, say,

'Please remind me of your name.'

That's all. It's direct, courteous and positive. It avoids that usual cumbersome, apologetic explanation: 'Oh, I'm terribly sorry, but I just can't seem to remember your name, although it's right on the tip of my tongue.' Leave out the embarrassment. There's no ignominy or disgrace about it. You've forgotten the name. You want to be reminded. That's all.

2. And If You Suspect They've Forgotten Yours ...
Self-assured, confident people announce their names when they see you. Even when the chances are that you will remember theirs, they make it easy for you. They begin a conversation by reaching out for your hand, and as

191

they shake it, say, 'I'm Heather White. We met at the information technology conference last year. It's nice to see you again.'

Your best bet when seeing someone who may have forgotten your name is to say,

'Hello, I'm _____**. It's nice to see you.'**

There's a built-in advantage to this approach: They'll probably respond with their own name, so if you've forgotten it you're already covered.

3. *When You Hear It, Use It.*

Most people don't really **forget** a name they used to remember, they just fail to remember it in the first place. Since names are vital in developing rapport and strengthening relationships, it's worth taking some simple steps to improve your name memorising techniques. The easiest thing to do is use a name as soon as you've heard it.

A not-very-successful salesman once said to me:

'Yes, George, I've been very successful in sales. And you know, George, it's really not difficult to do very, very well once you've mastered the basics. One of the things I always try to do is use the other person's name during the conversation. And as you well know, George, that's especially important on the phone. It really gets the other person's attention. But, George, you just can't please everyone. In fact, just the other day I talked to a man who, well, what he said, George, was, "You seem too smooth when you use my name too much." I kid you not, George . . . .'

Ouch! Screeching fingernails on a blackboard. I found myself counting how many times he said my name, wanting to interrupt and say, 'You idiot! Why didn't you listen to that other customer?'

Here's a simple guideline: *Use the other person's name three times in a conversation.* First, just after he says it. Second, sometime during the conversation, and third, as you end it.

Taking a couple of simple steps to ensure that you remember and use someone's name makes them feel good, and helps you feel good too.

Your business life and personal life are both based on personal relationships. Knowing and using people's names counts for a lot. Get into the habit of remembering and using them right from the start.

QUICK REFERENCE

What you can do right now:

Consciously use people's names three times during conversations. When you meet someone for the first time, immediately use his name and remember it. And when you see someone who may have forgotten your name, remind him straight away. If you've forgotten his, ask him to remind you.

Instead of saying,

'I'm sorry, it's on the tip of my tongue, but I just can't seem to think of your name.'

Say,

'Please remind me of your name.'

Instead of saying,

'You probably don't remember my name, but . . . .'

Say,

'Nice to see you again, my name's _____.'

Instead of saying,

'I'm sorry, but I just can't remember your name.'

Say,

'Hello, again. I'm _____. Please remind me of your name.'

48. *What's the Magic Word?*

It's Friday afternoon and your secretary has once again worked through lunch to be sure that your handouts are ready for your presentation first thing on Monday morning.
Say out loud to yourself:

'I don't know how I'd manage without Christine. I wish the rest of the secretarial staff were half as conscientious about deadlines as she is.'

Now say:

'Christine, thank you for doing such excellent work on the handouts, and for giving up your lunch hour. I'm very grateful for your dedication.'

Which version will ensure that Christine 'keeps up the good work'?

A retired neighbour of mine devotes much of her time to fund-raising for the American Cancer Society. She works tirelessly and has achieved great results that benefit many seriously ill patients.
Recently she phoned my wife in desperation.

'Julie, I've got a terrible problem. We're about to hold our biggest fund-raising event of the year and we don't have the air tickets promised in our promotional literature for the auction. Do you know anybody who could make a big donation? One or two air tickets would be ideal.'

My mother died of cancer, so I have a personal interest in wanting to help beat this disease. One of our best friends, Kevyn Leiner, was at that time a sales manager for USAir. He's a great friend and a generous person, so he was our 'target'. Time was very short, so the neighbour gave us a letter explaining about the auction, and we faxed it to USAir immediately. Within 48 hours Kevyn sent us two unrestricted free tickets anywhere in the USAir route system, worth up to $3000.

When the auction took place, Julie and I were away in England. We returned home, expecting to find a thank-you note and a copy of the American Cancer Society's formal letter to USAir and Kevyn. We found nothing.

Although we saw the neighbour from time to time, we never really stopped to talk to her. I felt somewhat resentful that she hadn't thanked Julie, who was responsible for initiating the airline contact in the first place, and whose friendly persuasion had encouraged Kevyn to donate the tickets.

Months later, I said to Kevyn,

'You know, that woman from the American Cancer Society never even had the courtesy to thank Julie for contacting you about the tickets you donated.'

Kevyn's response:

'Oh, they never thanked me either. It happens all the time. You'd be surprised at how many charitable organisations ask for contributions, neglect to say please, and then never follow up in any way.'

The point of the story is this: it's stupid and ungracious to overlook simple courtesies like saying please and expressing appreciation. After all the neighbour's hard work, the impression left with us, and with USAir's sales manager, is negative. I presume the tickets fetched a good price, and that the ACS benefited. The neighbour, though, will get a cool reception if she turns to USAir or to us next year.

She didn't mean to be rude, I'm sure. She just overlooked one of the basics. She allowed her hard work to be over-shadowed by a careless slip.

It's so easy, and so rare, to be genuinely courteous to people who mean a lot to us – especially customers. And the returns are phenomenal. A standard rule of thumb among sales professionals is that it costs at least five times as much to win an order from a new customer as it costs to win one from an existing customer. In my work as a sales adviser I've never found the figure to be that low. Organisations that have bothered to take a close look find it's at least ten times as costly to win new customers' business.

When I act as a consultant to marketing organisations, I often begin by asking,

> 'What are you doing to let your existing customers know that you appreciate them?'

The answer is nearly always revealing and embarrassing.

Sales forces typically invest huge amounts of time, money and personal energy chasing after new customers. And then they forget about them.

One of my most popular speaking topics deals with reducing customer 'churn'. I use the visual analogy of a conveyor belt. Picture a long conveyor belt about 3 feet wide, moving away from you at a steady speed. You're standing at the beginning of the belt, alongside a salesperson, and the belt moves away from you, off into the distance. In my speeches, I show three slides depicting that conveyor belt.

The first shows the eager, enthusiastic salesperson lavishing attention on a new customer – let's call him Harry – helping him step on to the belt. This corresponds to the most common, and most expensive, task in any marketing organisation: *winning new customers.* Using a combination of advertising, trade exhibition stands, direct mail campaigns, telemarketing calls, and often, face-to-face sales appointments, we set out to convince customers to buy something from us, to 'get them on the conveyor belt'.

My second slide shows the same conveyor belt. Now the salesperson is lavishing attention on another prospect, hoping to convert him into a customer. Harry has now progressed in his relationship – moved along on the conveyor belt. He may even have made a couple of repeat purchases. The salesperson, though, is concentrating his attention on the new prospect, seeking to get him on the belt and convert him into a customer. Meanwhile, our friend Harry is glancing at his watch, thinking,

'It's been a while since I got much attention from my salesperson. I was very important to him just before my first purchase and now I'm feeling taken for granted.'

The salesperson, of course, is hardly aware of Harry's feelings of being neglected. He's too busy winning new customers to pay much attention to the second big task in marketing: *Keeping customers on the conveyor belt.*

In the third slide, we see the same salesperson again. He's attentively convincing yet another new prospect to become a customer, to get on the conveyor belt. We see other customers who've recently begun their relationships with the company moving along into the distance, just as Harry did. And there's Harry, far down the belt, jumping off. He's going to jump on to a competitor's conveyor belt. They've been making him feel important and appreciated again.

Most salespeople completely neglect the third task in marketing: *Find out why customers are getting off your conveyor belt.*

An organisation's 'churn rate' refers to the rate at which new customers become disenchanted and fall off the conveyor belt. In every business, a customer relationship may be thought of as a stream of expected future cash flow. That's especially true of firms that depend on membership and subscription. It costs them (and every other type of business) a lot to win a new customer. Take cable TV, for example. If a customer signs up for cable service and then cancels just a few months later, the company will lose money on the account. To stay in business, it has to actively seek new customers to ensure an adequate future cash flow to cover its fixed expenses. When one of these customers cancels his cable service, and the company has to replace him, it's dealing with churn.

A high churn rate is extremely costly. Think of what happens when someone cancels their cable TV service. Several clerks are involved in closing the account and organising the paperwork. A service representative has to come to their home to sever the cable connection. The computers are reprogrammed to delete the account number. But those are just the obvious costs.

We've got to consider the cost of winning another new customer – of getting him on the conveyer belt – to replace the missing cash flow represented by the unhappy customer who has just jumped off. For a cable TV company, that means more advertising, direct mail and special incentives.

Why does churn happen? One of the most oft-repeated statistics on the seminar circuits of the late 1980s came from an American restaurant association. That study revealed that when a restaurant's patrons stop eating there and are asked why, they cite the following reasons:

1 per cent   *Died*
3 per cent   *Moved Away*
5 per cent   *Developed other relationships*
9 per cent   *Preferred a competitor*
14 per cent   *Were dissatisfied about the product (meal)*
68 per cent   *Felt an attitude of neglect or indifference*

I know of no wide-reaching national research to determine why customers fall off conveyer belts, but these percentages look pretty accurate to me. I've had several clients conduct expensive studies to get their own answers. The major reason is always the same: customers feel taken for granted.

Once marketing executives grasp the true costs of customer churn, they want to know the most effective way of reducing it – to keep customers on the conveyer belt longer. The easiest way is ridiculously simple: remember to say please and thank you.

It's so easy – and profitable – to improve customer retention in any business. You don't need to send expensive gifts or conceive a complicated customer appreciation campaign. A simple, sincere, personal thank you is all it takes.

Personal relationships can be very like customer relationships. Friendships and marriages can wither because of the same tendency to neglect common courtesies. You can easily apply the same 'conveyer belt principle' to your non-business relationships. Your success at building and maintaining any kind of relationship depends on the same three skills: initiating, nurturing, and recapturing. Whether it's your marriage, a close personal friendship, or a casual relationship with a neighbour, think in terms of getting them on the conveyor belt, keeping them on, and finding out what's wrong when they fall off.

Positive talkers remember the basics. They never fail to say please and thank you when it's the gracious thing to do. And they don't wait until it's expected. Every now and then they send a postcard, call a customer back, or drop in to thank a helpful neighbour. Parents who teach their children that 'please' and 'thank you' are magic words aren't exaggerating.

QUICK REFERENCE

What you can do right now:

Remember to exercise common courtesies in relationships with others, particularly those you're inclined to take for granted. Don't be stingy with 'please' and 'thank you'.

Instead of saying,

> 'Those people at the dry cleaners certainly do a good job.'

Say,

> **'Thank you for cleaning my clothes so well. I appreciate your excellent service.'**

Instead of saying,

> 'We've got to attract 1000 new customers this quarter.'

Say,

> **'I'm going to make absolutely sure our present customers know how much we appreciate them.'**

Instead of saying,

> 'My wife? Yes, she's great. She looks after the baby, cooks wonderful meals, keeps the house tidy and works hard. I'm lucky.'

Say,

> 'Darling, this weekend I'm going to do something special to let you know how much I appreciate you. Thank you for doing such a great job.'

Instead of saying,

> 'They know I appreciate them.'

Say,

> 'Thank you.'

49. *Say You're Sorry*

Following a company audit, the branch manager calls you to her office and asks about a meal receipt in your expenses that doesn't appear to have been business-related. Sure enough it turns out that you charged a family dinner to your company credit card three months ago.

Say out loud to yourself:

> 'With all the paperwork we have to do, I'm surprised there was only one mistake. I bet everybody here has a few personal meals slip through now and then. You can't blame me for making a mistake once in a while.'

Now say:

> 'You're absolutely right, that was a personal meal and it should not have been charged as a business expense. I'm sorry I didn't catch it myself and I will be extra careful in the future. It's my mistake and I apologise.'

Which sounds like the more trustworthy employee? Who will the branch manager be more likely to recommend for promotion?

In America most companies that handle a large number of customer calls now use an electronic device called an Automatic Call Distributor, or ACD.

One major advantage of an ACD is that it helps connect callers with exactly the right person. The ACD analyses each incoming call and quickly identifies which number the caller has dialled, what part of the country he's calling from, and in some cases, the specific telephone he's using. Then it directs his call to the member of staff who specialises in the questions he's most likely to ask. Telephone centre managers rely on ACDs because they provide very helpful statistical analyses of representatives' performances. For every employee, supervisory group, work shift, or hour of the day, the manager knows how many calls were made or answered, how long the average call lasted, how much time the rep spent processing paperwork, and so on.

Managers pay a great deal of attention to what's called the 'per cent time available/unavailable statistic'. When an individual rep is working efficiently, handling lots of calls with only very brief pauses between each one, his 'availability' to talk to customers is high. When a rep is procrastinating, taking an unnecessary length of time with his paperwork, chatting to colleagues, and avoiding customer contact, his ratio shows a high 'unavailable' percentage.

One of my clients' call centre managers decided to put a summary of all the reps' individual statistics on the departmental noticeboard. To avoid embarrassment, she substituted employee I.D. numbers for names. Two reps, Stanley and Stephanie, both checked the figures and noticed that their availability percentages were unfavourable. They were handling fewer calls (and taking longer to do it) than their colleagues.

As a consultant to many call centre managers, I have yet to discover a completely foolproof system for measuring perfomance (or allocating commissions, or scheduling work shifts fairly, or anything else). There's always someone who will get round whatever system the management implements.

Stanley got round the ACD in his call centre. He worked out that the device counts how many minutes his phone is busy, how many calls he handles, and how long his conversations last. It doesn't 'listen in' to see who he's talking to or even if he's talking at all.

So Stanley started calling his home number and letting the phone ring for three minutes, then hanging up and calling again, and then hanging up and calling again. The ACD counted each as a customer call. The next time statistics were posted on the board, Stanley's performance showed dramatic improvement! The average number of calls he handled each day had soared from 47 to 92! According to the statistics, he was on the phone almost all the time. His average call length was exactly the same as the average for other reps. He appeared to be very productive.

Stephanie, a new employee, had been struggling to improve her performance statistics. Then Stanley showed her how to do it. Overnight, her figures also showed an amazing improvement.

Of course the manager noticed these dramatic changes and asked both employees what was going on.

Stephanie admitted what she had done, accepted personal responsibility, apologised, and stopped doing it. Her performance continues to improve legitimately and she has a bright future with her employer.

Stanley blamed his performance on the pressured environment. That ended is employment.

When I was a student at the University of California I landed a dream job. I was taken on as the Trans World Airlines campus sales representative. The money wasn't much; the benefits, though, were incredible! As a 20-year-old student with an unlimited air travel pass, I asked myself each week:

> 'Shall I stay on campus this weekend, spend a couple of dollars at the theatre, and a few more on meals. Or shall I catch a flight to London, see two films going over and two more coming back, enjoy four nice in-flight meals, sightsee for a few hours in England, and spend nothing?'

I didn't spend many weekends on campus.

As an airline sales representative, you inevitably deal with some of your customers just after they've returned from a terrible flight on your airline. I remember being verbally assaulted by the men's choir director after he'd taken his boys on a European tour. I escorted them as far as Frankfurt, then bade the group farewell as they went off to sing in several European capitals. Meanwhile I headed off to visit a friend in Berlin before returning home.

Two weeks later, back on campus, I was blasted by the director:

'I'll never fly on TWA again! Your airline lost our entire group's luggage on the flight from Rome to Paris. You cancelled our flight from Madrid to LA and instead sent us home via Lisbon, Philadelphia and Kansas City. What have you got to say?'

My boss and mentor at TWA was Paul Oglesby, an ex-professional footballer. One of the most important lessons he taught me was:

'When you're wrong, make no excuses. Say sincerely, "You are absolutely right and I don't blame you for feeling upset. I'm sorry we messed things up".'

After the choir director's tirade had reached its crescendo, I followed Paul's advice and sincerely apologised without making excuses. The following year the men's choir again flew TWA on its European tour.

When the Chrysler Corporation was accused of resetting new car odometers back to zero after executives had driven them for personal use, what did Chairman Lee Iacocca do? He admitted the truth, made no excuses, apologised personally on the company's behalf, and offered to pay compensation to those owners whose 'new' cars really hadn't been unused. Dishonesty cost the company at least $26 million in penalties and settlements. Criminal fines alone could have exceeded $100 million if the Chairman had not chosen to be forthright. But he told the truth. As a result, the company's performance remained strong in the face of the potentially devastating publicity, and the Chairman bolstered his image as an honest person.

Follow Paul Oglesby's advice: when you are personally wrong, or when the organisation you represent has mistreated a customer it's always best to admit the mistake, accept responsibility, apologise, promise to do everything you can to correct it, and immediately start doing so.

QUICK REFERENCE

What you can do right now:

Whenever you make a mistake, admit it readily and say you're sorry. Defuse potential explosions, avoid confrontations, and build others' respect for your character by facing facts, admitting the truth, and apologising.

Instead of saying to yourself,

> 'With all these people drinking red wine, he'll never know that I'm the one who stained his new sofa. He probably won't even notice it until the morning.'

Say,

> **'Bill, I'm sorry, but I spilled wine on your sofa. Let's put some stain remover or soda water on it straight away before it sets overnight.'**

Instead of saying,

> 'Don't blame me if the client files are out of order. Other people use them too, you know.'

Say,

> **'I'm sorry you had trouble finding the client file you wanted. I'll go through and check them all before Friday.'**

Instead of saying,

> 'Look, it's just too bad. Don't blame me. I couldn't help it.'

Say,

> **'I'm sorry; it was my responsibility.'**

IX. *Share Your Pride*

A TRULY positive talker is not content to bolster his own image and self-esteem, he makes sure that he's enriching those of others, too.

I began writing this book with an underlying mission. My drive sprang from a need I have experienced personally. Thinking back, I now realise that many of my choices in life have been motivated by one desire: to be acknowledged and applauded. I've found that I'm not alone.

This last chapter is my most important message to you.

50. *The Sound of One Man Clapping*

You've just read the draft version of a long-term strategic plan for your organisation prepared by an inter-departmental project team you put together. It's outstanding.

Say out loud to yourself:

'This is the strategic plan my project team have developed. They've done an excellent job; it's the best plan we've ever had. They should be feeling pretty pleased with themselves.'

Now say:

'I'm proud of every one of you who worked on this project. You've done an excellent job, and I'm going to make sure that the boss knows exactly how proud of you I am. After I've gone through it with her, I'll tell you exactly what she said. For now, I want you to know that your excellent and hard work is very evident. Thank you.'

Which sounds like the leader whose team members will feel that their work is truly appreciated? Who's making a big mistake by assuming that his team feels appreciated?

My dad, Merle Walther, was born in 1908 and grew up in Sacramento, California. His large family – five children, of whom my dad was the youngest – didn't have much money. Dad did have a talent for playing baseball. He was well known in the local leagues and was apparently a terrific first baseman. So good in fact that a scout from Detroit recruited him to play professionally. Dad thinks of the afternoon when that scout came to his house as a near-religious experience. He imagined how proud his family would be as he became a famous baseball star.

Sitting in the humble front room, the scout asked for permission to take Merle back to Detroit so he could join the team. Dad recalls what his father said:

'I've heard about those baseball players. They drink. They smoke. They chase women. And after a few years, their careers are over. I won't hear of it. My son's going to go to college.'

Dad was heartbroken, but there was no arguing. After all, Grandpa was a German 'head of the household', and when he said NO, that was that. I'm sure Dad resented his father's decree all his life. He yearned to play baseball.

Sure enough Dad went off to college and did quite well studying electronics. He got a good job with the Pacific Telephone and Telegraph Company and specialised in microwave transmissions.

When World War II broke out, he volunteered to join the Navy and became a radar officer on a destroyer escort in the South Pacific. I'm sure he played a lot of baseball on the Navy teams when they were ashore.

And then, after the war, I was born. What do you suppose Dad wanted me to do? That's right. Play baseball.

As a kid, I remember Dad constantly playing catch with me in the front garden. For me it wasn't fun, it was torture. But Dad wanted me to be the baseball star his father hadn't let him become. He forced me to sign up for Little League.

I showed an early leaning towards sales. Neighbours and family friends all said I had the gift of the gab. I always sold the most raffle tickets and started a succession of local sales enterprises peddling greeting cards, firewood, extension leads, trivets and used comic books. I could succeed in selling anything. Baseball just interfered with my sales activities.

I don't recall Dad ever congratulating me for being such a good little salesman. He often pointed out that his son was a disappointing baseball player.

Finally I summoned up the courage to tell Dad that I would not join Little League the following season. So he joined, as the chief umpire. Poor Dad. He must have felt terribly ashamed when the other umpires asked why his son didn't play for one of the teams.

Through my high school years, Dad continued to volunteer as a Little League umpire. I continued to avoid team sports. I was now winning sales contests and being chosen by my high school peers to head our model companies. Dad didn't acknowledge my business acumen, he just wished I would play baseball.

At high school graduation, I received many academic and service honours, but none for athletics. Dad pointed that out too.

At university, I majored in Rhetoric and Public Address, and graduated *summa cum laude*. Dad didn't say he was proud, only that he wished I had at least tried to get into the college baseball team.

Later on, I'd phone Dad to tell him how well I was doing with my business administration classes and he'd try to tell me how well the San Francisco Giants were doing. Finally he'd give up, saying, 'Of course you don't give a damn about baseball. You never have.'

Years later, when I completed my first book, *Phone Power,* it struck me that of all the subjects I could have written a book about, I had chosen telephones. Dad had by now retired from a 40-year career with a telephone company. It seemed I was doing everything I could to win his approval. Except play baseball.

When the publisher sent me my first copy of the book, fresh from the printer, I inscribed it to Dad and sent it to him.

'Dad, you may never realise how much of my business success has been the result of striving to make you proud of me.'

As I complete this book that you're reading, Dad still hasn't read *Phone Power,* and he hasn't once commented on my inscription.

A few years ago I presented a speech in San Francisco and invited Dad to be my guest in the audience. He'd had many opportunities before, but hadn't come. Even now, as a retired, lonely man (my mother had died some years earlier), he said that he probably wouldn't make it to my speech. Although he was in superb health, and the hotel was less than half an hour from his home, he complained that:

> 'Parking's impossible in San Francisco. And I'm not going to pay some damned valet car parker three or four bucks just to park my car.'

Well, Dad did show up. And I was in top form. As I ended my presentation, Dad stood up and began to applaud, biting his lower lip. I've enjoyed many wonderful ovations, but none was ever as loud as the sound of that one man clapping.

My eyes moisten, right now as I type, as I remember how I felt when Dad said the words I'd yearned to hear all my life:

> 'Son, I'm proud of you.'

Whenever I share that story with my audiences, several people come up the stage at the end. Their eyes are red and they say,

> 'My mother/father was just like that. She/he never did say "I'm proud of you," though I wanted very much to hear it. What is it about our parents that makes it so hard for them to say it?'

Once I've opened up, others do. And it turns out that we're all very much alike. As I tell the story of my dad and his wanting me to be something I'm not, I see many in the audience reacting emotionally. Instead of approaching me after the applause, I hope they go directly to the call boxes in the lobby and phone the people they're proud of.

It's remarkable how common this striving for appreciation is. In Kirk Douglas's autobiography, *Ragman's Son,* he traces most of his life's achievements back to his struggle to be noticed and appreciated by his father. He never got the satisfaction of hearing his dad say that he was.

After a decade of strained relations, my dad and I got together at last. The speech in San Francisco, when he finally said 'I'm proud of you', was a milestone in our relationship. When I explained how much I wanted him to be proud of me, his response was,

'You must be kidding. Since the day you were born, I've been telling every friend I have how proud I am of you. Don't you know that?'

Well, now I know. And it feels great.

I've always thought my career choice is quite revealing. I stand on stage before hundreds or thousands of people, working hard to earn their appreciation. For years, their ovations helped compensate for my dad's failure to tell me that he was proud of me.

You can be sure that most of the people you'll ever meet are striving to be noticed and applauded. It's a natural instinct, and one that goes unfulfilled in many. The people you know and work with are hungry for appreciation. They're probably not getting enough of it from the people they love.

If you do nothing else after reading this book, please phone the people you love and tell them why you're proud of them. Do it now.

QUICK REFERENCE

What you can do right now:

Let the people you feel proud of hear about it.

Instead of saying,

'My daughter is a wonderful student. Everyone likes her. And she's so beautiful. I'm proud of her.'

Say,

'Sweetheart, I'm very proud of you. You're a wonderful student, you have some great friends, and you're gorgeous.'

Instead of saying,

'Gordon has a great future here. He's doing excellent work in my department, and I suspect he'll be off to head office in a year or two. He should feel very proud of himself.'

Say,

'Gordon, you are handling your career very well, and
your work is very valuable to the company. I know you
have an excellent future here. I'm proud of you.'

Instead of saying,

'Our organisation does a great job arranging superb
workshops that help a lot of people.'

Say,

'Barbara, since you've been the executive director of our
association, we've never had a finer management team.
I want you to know that I'm proud to be a member of
our association.'

Instead of saying,

'I'm sure he knows I'm proud of him.'

Say,

'I'm proud of you.'

X. *DO IT NOW*

POSITIVE talking affects every aspect of your life – **once you start using it.**

There are three critical steps in becoming a positive talker: (1) Decide you're going to change, (2) Build a support system to keep you on course, and (3) Monitor your progress to keep up the momentum.

1. Decide to Be a Positive Talker
Choose to project a more positive image, encourage others to cooperate with you, accelerate your career progress, and enjoy more positive, fulfilling relationships.

As you read the examples in this book, you'll notice that they're all very down-to-earth. You don't need to be a high-flying executive to benefit from positive talking. These principles work whether you are a salesperson, a supervisor, someone who's just starting your career, or an established leader of your organisation – and they're just as beneficial for parents, friends, consumers and anyone else.

Are the techniques difficult to master? Certainly not. There are no new words to learn and there's nothing complicated about applying the principles.

Once you make the decision, the action is easy.

2. Build a Support System
Teaming up with a partner is the single most important thing you can do. Invite someone you work with, live with, or enjoy a strong friendship with to become a positive talker too. There's nothing like a companion who's listening for

negative phrases that may slip out during your conversations. Agree to help each other by remaining vigilant about each other's language. You could use a subtle reminder like winking or clearing your throat, or you could be a lot more conspicuous. Some positive talkers write the powerless phrases they're purging on wide rubber bands and wear them round their wrists. When their partners hear them slip, SNAP!

For best results, form two or more partnerships covering your professional and personal lives. If you have children at home, help prepare them for the real world by sharing the positive talking principles. It only takes a little incentive to enlist their zealous support in cleansing your vocabulary. Offer a child 10 pence every time he catches you saying 'but' instead of 'and', and you'll soon break old habits.

3. Monitor Your Progress
You will notice the difference positive talking makes in your daily life, and you'll also become very aware of powerless talkers around you. Each time you hear someone say, 'To be honest with you', or 'I was just lucky', or 'I'd hate to', or 'I'll try', you'll notice the negative impression that phrase makes on anyone listening. And that will serve as a reminder to keep up your own steady progress.

All 50 positive talking phrases are summarised in the 'Quick Reference' section that follows. As you master each one, note your successes and reward yourself. Remember, though, that positive talking isn't a final destination at which you arrive. It's a continuing journey, so enjoy your trip.

I've enjoyed my journey while writing this book, and have benefited tremendously from the process of listening for examples and translating them into principles. Thank you for reading.

More Power to You!

George R. Walther

QUICK REFERENCE SUMMARY

Use the following pages as a quick reference summary to remind you of the 50 positive talking techniques.

I. PROJECT POSITIVE EXPECTATIONS

1. I'll Be Glad To!

Each time you begin to say 'I'll **have to,**' substitute a phrase that shows you'll be **glad to.** Notice the difference it makes in your own mood and in others' attitudes towards cooperating with you.

Instead of saying,

'I'll have to do it.'

Say,

'I'll be glad to do it.'

2. Will You Try, or Will You DO It?

Tell yourself and everyone else what you **will** do, not what you'll **try** to do.

Instead of saying,

'I'll try to do it.'

Say,

'I will do it.'

3. Say What You Want to Do

Use 'I want to' to describe the positive outcome you envisage, rather than saying what you'd 'hate to' have happen.

Instead of saying,

'I'd hate to give you the wrong information.'

Say,

'I want to help you get the right information.'

4. *I Haven't Yet and I CAN*

When describing your capabilities to yourself or to someone else, eliminate 'I can't' from your vocabulary.
Instead of saying,

'I can't do that.'

Say,

'I haven't yet done it and I can.'

5. *Refuse to Be Helpless*

If you feel sick, combine appropriate medical attention with personal action. Use your language to promote a positive attitude and strengthen your body's natural disease-fighting powers.
Instead of saying,

'My condition is hopeless; I can't change it.'

Say,

'I can improve the quality of my life.'

6. *Better When Than If*

When you hear yourself starting to ask a conditional 'If ...' question, rephrase it to incorporate your positive expectation.
Instead of saying,

'I was wondering if you could ...?'

Say,

'When will you ...?'

7. *It's No Problem!*

Substitute 'challenge' or 'opportunity' for 'problem' and concentrate on exploring solutions.
Instead of saying,

'I'm afraid that's going to be a problem.'

Say,

'That sounds like a challenging opportunity.'

8. *Self-Fulfilling Prophecies Come True*

Replace habitual self-limiting phrases with empowering assertions.
Instead of saying,

'I'm no good at that.'

Say,

'I'm getting better at that.'

9. *Get a Return on Your Investments*

Substitute 'invest' for 'spend' when you talk about how you plan to use your time, money and other resources.
Instead of saying,

'I'm going to spend some time and money taking evening classes.'

Say,

'I'm going to invest some time and money in taking evening classes so I'm ready to move ahead in my career.'

10. *Nothing's Impossible*

Banish the word 'impossible' from your vocabulary. Substitute a more accurate and positive phrase to describe what appears infeasible.
Instead of saying,

'This is impossible.'

Say,

'This is going to require a special effort, and it can be done.'

11. *Kids Are All Ears*

Be especially conscious of positive talking whenever you are with young people. Set an example and help shape children's futures by speaking positively to and about them.
Instead of saying,

'You're a bad child and you're always getting into trouble.'

Say,

'You're a good child, and that behaviour is not acceptable.'

II. GIVE CREDIT WHERE IT'S DUE

12. *What's Your Excuse?*

Stop making excuses and apologising for some imagined shortcoming. Either change it or forget it.
Instead of saying,

'You'll have to excuse my car/mess/hair/house.'

Say,

Nothing!

13. *It's Just My Opinion*

You're not 'just' or 'only' anything. Describe yourself, your beliefs and your accomplishments positively and proudly.
Instead of saying,

'I'm only the . . . .'

Say,

'I am the . . . .'

14. *Is 'Luck' Getting the Credit for Your Hard Work?*

When you succeed, modestly acknowledge your own role in attaining your accomplishments, both to yourself and to others.

Instead of saying,

'I was lucky.'

Say,

'I planned well and worked hard.'

15. *What They Don't Know Won't Hurt Them*

You're probably far more critical of yourself than anybody else will be. Go ahead and enjoy doing as well as you can.

Instead of saying,

'I'm really not very good at this.'

Do your best without making excuses.

16. *Catch People Doing Things Right*

Go out of your way to compliment people and give them credit for doing things right, especially when they don't expect it.

Instead of saying,

'My daughter is a big help round the house.'

Say,

'Darling, you are a big help round the house, and I appreciate it.'

17. *You're About as Old as You Say You Are*

Use neutral or positive phrases when talking about advancing age. Don't erode vitality by speaking negatively about aging.

Instead of saying,

'I feel worse and worse. I'm getting old.'

Say,

'I feel good.'

III. REBOUND RESILIENTLY

18. Does Your History Repeat Itself?

When you're confronted with a 'failure', look for the lessons you can learn, and grow from the experience.
Instead of saying,

'I failed.'

Say,

'Here's what I learned . . . .'

19. Half-Empty or Half-Full?

Rephrase negative reactions to unexpected changes and say, 'This is great news. It means that . . . ,' and then start looking for the positive result that can follow.
Instead of saying,

'I see some very negative consequences resulting from this turn of events.'

Say,

'I see some very positive consequences resulting from this turn of events.'

20. If Only I Had . . .

Focus your attention – and your language – on what you will do to shape your future positively. Don't dwell on the unalterable past by talking about what might have been.
Instead of saying,

'If only I had.'

Say,

'Starting now, I will.'

21. *Bottoming Out*

When you're at a low point, write out your affirmations, using positive language, and say them aloud to yourself. Don't just think, act.

Instead of thinking to yourself,

'I'm a loser.'

Say,

'I am a winner.'

22. *Bouncing Back*

When you hear yourself describing a setback as a complete disaster, rephrase your description to recognise that you will bounce back and move on.

Instead of saying,

'I'm going under.'

Say,

'I'm going to bounce back.'

23. *It's Over!*

When things seem to be moving towards a disastrous outcome, stop and ask yourself, 'What's the very worst that could happen?' Accept that eventuality as if it were true and say, 'That's all; it's over.' Then start using your energy to create a more positive outcome.

Instead of saying,

'This is terrible, and it could get a lot worse.'

Say,

'Even if the worst happened, I could live with it. So there's no point worrying. *That's all; it's over.* Now I'm going to start making things better.'

221

IV. ACCEPT RESPONSIBILITY

24. Watch Where You Point That Thing!

Be on the lookout for that pointing finger! Whenever you hear (or see) yourself directing blame or responsibility elsewhere, focus on the three fingers that point back at you.
Instead of saying,

'You upset me when . . . .'

Say,

'I feel upset when . . . .'

25. Use the Time You Have

Get rid of phrases that suggest time is out of your control – that there's not enough of it. Acknowledge your personal responsibility with your language.
Instead of saying,

'I just can't catch up; I don't have enough time.'

Say,

'I can catch up by managing my time and eliminating less important projects.'

26. It's Not What Happens to You, It's What You Do About It

Accept personal responsibility for your present situation and decide to move forward rather than wasting energy by blaming your current condition on past circumstances.
Instead of saying,

'I can't help it; it's someone else's fault.'

Say,

'It's my responsibility to change things.'

27. *You Can Count on Me*

Even though you may not be the person who will actually perform the task, accept personal responsibility when you offer to help someone.
Instead of saying,

'That's not my area. You'll have to get someone else to help you.'

Say,

'I'll help you by passing your message on to the right department.'

28. *Do You Choose to Lose?*

Avoid 'victim' language; acknowledge your responsibility by using the word 'choose'. When you're dissatisfied with the way things are, choose to change them.
Instead of saying,

'I can't change things, I didn't get myself into this situation.'

Say,

'I choose to make the best of this situation.'

V. ENCOURAGE COOPERATION AND REDUCE CONFLICT

29. *Get That 'But' Out of Your Mouth!*

Make a conscious decision to replace 'but' with 'and' when you talk to yourself and to others. Notice how your thinking 'opens up' as ideas coexist instead of conflict.
Instead of saying,

'I can see that it's a good product, but it's expensive.'

Say,

'I can see that it's a good product, and it's expensive.'

30. *Let's Do It!*

Whenever you seek others' input and suggestions, stimulate a free flow of ideas, no matter how crazy some of them might seem.

Instead of saying,

'That's not practical, it'll never work.'

Say,

'That's an unusual approach, let's think about it and see where it leads.'

31. *Do ME a Favour for a Change*

When you need someone's cooperation, work out how his participation will benefit him, not you. Emphasise the benefits he'll gain by following your suggestion.

Instead of saying,

'Will you do me a favour?'

Say,

'Here's how this will benefit you.'

32. *You Get What You Ask For*

Make it a habit to ask at least one relationship-improving question every day.

Instead of saying,

'Is everything satisfactory?'

Say,

'How can I do a better job?'

33. *So, What CAN You Do?*

Whenever you start telling someone what you can't do, change your focus and substitute a statement indicating what you can do.

Instead of saying,

'Here's what I can't do.'

Say,

'Here's what I can do.'

34. *Breaking the Language Barrier*

When you're involved in a conflict, use your language to show that you're intent on working *with,* not *against* the other person; show that you're on the same side, working together.
Instead of saying,

'I understand what you want. But I have to stick to my policies.'

Say,

'We share some important goals. Let's see how we can work together.'

35. *You're Invited!*

When you want others to cooperate with you, 'invite' them to do so, and give them a choice about what they'll do.
Instead of saying,

'Here's what you'll have to do.'

Say,

'I invite you to choose the approach that will work best for you.'

36. *I Recommend*

Whenever you set out to 'sell' an idea, service or product, focus on the benefits to the other person and use the word 'recommend' to close the sale.
Instead of saying,

'One thing you might possibly want to consider is to . . . .'

Say,

'I recommend that you . . . .'

37. What Sounds Fair to You?

Whenever you feel that people are about to treat you unjustly, appeal to their own sense of fairness. In the few cases where they continue to act unfairly, forget about it.
Instead of saying,

'I know my rights, and I demand that you do the following.'

Say,

'Considering the facts, what would be the fairest way to handle this?'

38. Let's Look at This Another Way

Rather than suggesting that someone else's viewpoint is less valid than your own, accept new ideas and let them coexist alongside yours. Then tap the merits of both approaches and come up with an even better alternative.
Instead of saying,

'I disagree with you.'

Say,

'I understand, and I'd like to consider some other viewpoints.

VI. SPEAK DECISIVELY

39. You Should – Or You WILL?

Commit yourself to specific dates, times and amounts. 'Should' avoids commitment and sounds wishy-washy.
Instead of saying,

'We should get this done by . . . .'

Say,

'We will get this done by . . . .'

40. *Give Your Word and Then Beat It!*

Add a 'safety cushion' whenever you make a commitment. Then delight the other person by doing your best to exceed the expectation you've created.
Instead of saying,

'I may be able to get to it by 2 or 3 p.m.'

Say,

'I will do it before 5 p.m.'

41. *I Think I Understand What You Think You Said*

Take an extra moment to check that you have understood accurately. Do it in a way that shows you accept responsibility for getting the information right.
Instead of saying,

'I suppose that covers it. I think we understand each other.'

Say,

'Let's check that we're in complete agreement by recapping on what we've discussed.'

42. *Don't Take 'No' – or 'Yes' – for an Answer*

Whenever you ask someone a question, first ask yourself, 'Is this a Yes/No question?' If it is, change it to the multiple-choice or open-ended variety.
Instead of saying,

'Do you have any questions?'

Say,

'What questions do you have?'

43. *Say It!*

Know what you want to say and say it!
Instead of saying,

'Well, generally speaking, one thing I would sort of tend to think is . . .'

Say,

'I believe . . . .'

VII. TELL THE TRUTH

44. To Be Honest with You

When everything you say *is* totally honest, there's no need to warn anyone that you're about to tell the truth. Eliminate integrity-destroying expressions that suggest you aren't always sincere.

Instead of saying,

'Well, to tell you the truth . . . .'

ALWAYS tell the truth.

45. Just Say No!

Before you agree to do anything you're only half sure you want to do, stop and think. Decide if you'll be able to do a good job, enjoy doing it, and finish it without interrupting your other more important priorities. If you decide that you don't really want to do it, say no.

Instead of saying,

'I don't really want to, but I suppose I'll say yes.'

Say,

'No, I won't, though I appreciate your asking.'

46. Never Say Always

Be alert for and eliminate universal terms like 'always', 'never', 'everything' and 'nothing', especially when using them to criticise someone else's performance or your own.

Instead of saying to yourself,

'Everything goes wrong **whenever** I try to negotiate with him. I **always** lose out and I **never** get treated fairly.'

Say,

'**Sometimes my negotiating techniques haven't resulted in a positive outcome. Next time I'm going to use another approach.**'

VIII. GET BACK TO BASICS

47. The Name Game

Consciously use people's names three times during conversations. When you meet someone for the first time, immediately use his name and remember it. And when you see someone who may have forgotten your name, remind him straight away. If you've forgotten his, ask him to remind you.

Instead of saying,

'I'm sorry, but I just can't seem to remember your name.'

Say,

'**Hello again. I'm _____. Please remind me of your name.**'

48. What's the Magic Word?

Remember to exercise common courtesies in relationship with others, particularly those you may take for granted. Don't be stingy with 'please' and 'thank you'.

Instead of saying,

'They know I appreciate them.'

Say,

'**Thank you.**'

49. Say You're Sorry

Whenever you make a mistake, admit it readily and say you're sorry. Defuse potential explosions, avoid confrontations, and build others' respect for your character by facing facts, admitting the truth, and apologising.

Instead of saying,

'Look, it's just too bad. Don't blame me. I couldn't help it.'

Say,

'I'm sorry; it was my responsibility.'

IX. SHARE YOUR PRIDE

50. The Sound of One Man Clapping

Let the people you feel proud of hear about it.

Instead of saying,

'I'm sure he knows I'm proud of him.'

Say,

'I'm proud of you.'

AN INVITATION FROM THE AUTHOR

To arrange customised Positive Talking or Phone Power presentations for your organisation, I invite you to call my office 24 hours a day on 001 – 206 – 255 – 2900. I'm proud to offer presentations for leading corporations and associations worldwide. I am honoured to hold the National Speakers Association's highest award for speaking skills and professionalism, the CPAE, as well as being a Certified Professional Speaker,

Many highly effective support materials are available to help you implement positive talking throughout your organisaion and in your personal life. They include audio and video cassette tapes suitable for corporate training and individual use, plus easy-to-use quick reference cards and progress-tracking systems.

For a fax brochure describing Positive Talking and Phone Power support materials, please fax your request to: 001 – 206 – 235 – 6360 and include a return fax number and address.

I'm now gathering ideas for 50 **more** positive talking techniques and look forward to hearing your examples. I'll be pleased to credit you when they're used in the next edition.

George R. Walther
6947 Coal Creek Parkway, Suite 100
Renton, WA 98059, USA
001 – 206 – 255 – 2900   Fax: 001 – 206 – 235 – 6360
Email: GeoWalther @ AOL.COM

Piatkus Books

If you have enjoyed this book you may be interested in other Piatkus books about communications:

Confident Conversation: *How to talk in any business or social situation* Dr Lillian Glass

Your Total Image: *How to communicate success* Philippa Davies

NLP: *The new art and science of getting what you want* Dr Harry Alder

NLP for Managers: *How to achieve excellence at work* Dr Harry Alder

For a free brochure with further information on our complete range of titles please write to:

Piatkus Books
Freepost 7 (WD 4505)
London W1E 4EZ